RUSHING
FOR
GOLD

Edited by John Walton Caughey

PACIFIC COAST BRANCH OF THE
AMERICAN HISTORICAL ASSOCIATION

Special Publication No. 1

UNIVERSITY OF CALIFORNIA PRESS
Berkeley and Los Angeles · 1949

UNIVERSITY OF CALIFORNIA PRESS
BERKELEY AND LOS ANGELES
CALIFORNIA

❖

CAMBRIDGE UNIVERSITY PRESS
LONDON, ENGLAND

Reprinted from the
PACIFIC HISTORICAL REVIEW
VOL. XVIII • NUMBER 1 • FEBRUARY, 1949

PRINTED IN THE UNITED STATES OF AMERICA
BY THE UNIVERSITY OF CALIFORNIA PRESS

CONTENTS

RUSHING FOR GOLD

T HE PAPERS *here assembled celebrate the centennial of the California gold rush. For background they have, of course, Marshall's
discovery at Coloma in January, 1848, the slow spread of interest
in this find, mounting in the summer to an epidemic of gold fever in
California and most other Pacific lands. In the more immediate background is the fabulous mining season of '48, characterized by most primitive technology and by equally fabulous returns. Toward the end of the
year the news belatedly gained credence in the States. Officially reported
by California's military governor, underwritten by samples delivered
by navy and army couriers, and officially received by the President of the
United States, the news touched off an eastern gold fever as devastating
as that which the West had felt. Out of that force came the rush.*

*No sheaf of papers such as this can tell all that there is to know about
that epic drama. The forty-niners themselves took seriously the challenge
of recording the history that they were making, as is suggested by the
thousands of letters and the hundreds of diaries and journals which are
its voluminous sources. Contemporary publishers, of newspapers and of
books, were equally avid for news from the Argonauts. Over the years
the interest of writers and publishers—and presumably of readers—has
persisted, with the result that the literature on the gold rush is now one
of the longest shelves in the whole field of western Americana.*

*To that shelf the papers that follow are, we hope, a contribution in
detail. They begin with attention to the main overland route, first in
terms of the pioneering of a route for wagons across the Sierra Nevada
at Donner Pass, and second in a picture of the towns where the emigrants
outfitted for the trail. Attention then shifts to the alternate southern
routes in an El Paso-to-California diary and in a résumé of the experiences of the Argonauts who crossed Mexico.*

*The other two main highways for gold seekers are represented in a
detailed analysis of the Panama crossing and in a characterization of the
ports of call frequented by those other forty-niners who elected the Cape
Horn route. In appropriate reflection of 1849 more space is accorded to
travel to California than to life in the diggings.*

*There are discussions, however, of four features of the California scene:
(1) a secret society organized and reorganized for the solace of the men of
these diggings; (2) the superb clippers that ran on the frieght route which*

in the golden era was California's chief economic tie to the civilized world; (3) the heroic labors of Protestant churchmen, whose fame is sometimes obscured by that of the more numerous saloonkeepers and gamblers; and (4) the incidence of disease and the beginnings of facilities to cope with problems of health.

Still other phases of the gold rush story might have had attention. The gold rush was a stimulant to things cultural, particularly to literature. And, of course, there were forty-niners who mined. These two activities are symbolized in a bit from the pen of Mark Twain, which also catches the brash and frolicking spirit of the forty-niners, of which every work on the subject should have at least a tinge.

When originally broached, the plan for this symposium included twice as many contributions on a longer and more varied list of topics. Some of the titles proposed—for example, "The Forty-niners as Political Scientists," and "Susanna and Her Sisters"—looked to me enticing. These eleven, however, were the ones destined for fruition. As I measure it, they are a tidy and useful addition to the literature on the gold rush.

JOHN WALTON CAUGHEY

Facts About the Blazing of the Gold Trail, Including a Few Never Before Published

IRENE D. PADEN

[Author of *In the Wake of the Prairie Schooner* (New York, 1943) and editor of *The Journal of Madison Berryman Moorman, 1850–1851* (San Francisco, 1948), Irene D. Paden of Alameda, California, is a prime expert on the overland trails.]

IT WAS APRIL on the Missouri River. The year was 1844. In a week or two the grass would sprout on the prairies and the Murphy-Stevens-Townsend party would start west across the almost trackless, treeless waste known as Indian territory.

The Murphy-Stevens-Townsend party was going to California with wagons. It never had been done. It had been attempted twice, but both the venturesome companies had been forced to leave their wagons along the way, to the utter amazement of the western Shoshone tribes that the white man should be so wasteful with his horse-canoes.

The three families who lent their names to the company had three very different reasons for the journey. Dr. Townsend and his in-laws, the Schallenbergers, were conducting a commercial enterprise and had several wagons filled with salable goods for the markets of California. The Murphys were devout Catholics and were heading for one of the mission valleys of the Pacific Coast where they might find a church of their own faith. The Stevens family, as well as the majority of the other families comprising the party, were seeking relief from the malarial climate of the Missouri Valley.

The company was well-knit and efficient, qualities definitely on the credit side of the ledger; the continued existence of such a party might well hang on its quick and concerted action in an emergency. Beyond this, the group had an asset which they may not have appreciated at first glance. It was a grizzled and wiry mountaineer, Caleb Greenwood, lately called the white chief of the Crow Nation. With him were six of his half-Indian offspring, ranging from John, twenty-two and married, to a little girl of six.

"Old Greenwood" admitted eighty-one years and was tough as a hickory ox yoke. He had been proud of his faithful Crow wife, recently deceased, but wanted to raise his children in the manner of the white race. He was used to the country of the Crows—of all Indian nations' the most beautiful—lying along the high eastern slopes of the Wind River Mountains. The feverish frontier along the Missouri bottoms displeased him, and he decided to try the much-talked-about new land of California, lauded as the most magnificent coast that ever laid an edge in salt water. The trip, too, would suit him. He was too full of vim to stagnate on a frontier that was getting past its prime. So he joined the migration of 1844.

He joined as an emigrant. But he agreed to act as guide as far as the Rockies. Beyond that, said Caleb, he did not know the road. True, he did not know it. But as unerringly as if he were a robot guided by a master hand pushing buttons, Old Greenwood found watercourses, canyons, passes, and took his company west apparently by remote control.

The wagons had not yet descended the last slope of the Rockies when Caleb improved the regular Oregon Trail by pioneering the short cut which was known for a few years by his name and was afterward called Sublette's Cutoff. Old Caleb never stayed with an undesirable section of trail simply because it was in use. Trusting to his Indian-trained woodcraft, he plotted another route and unhesitatingly took the clumsy wagons by the new way. Probably half of the overland forty-niners made use of this daring short cut across Green River Desert.

The party struck Bear River in the vicinity of what is now Cokeville and kept on the Oregon Trail as far as Fort Hall, where the major problem of the journey had to be faced: in what direction should they proceed to insure safe arrival with their wagons? The two California-bound companies which had preceded the 1844 group were the Bidwell-Bartleson company in 1841 and the Chiles-Walker party in 1843. The former had turned southwest at the great bend of Bear River and had abandoned their wagons, beyond any reasonable doubt, near the spring on what is now the Johnson Ranch in Steptoe Valley, Nevada. The other party had remained with the regular trail at least as far as Fort Hall, where the company divided. Chiles took a small pack train and continued with the trail as far as Fort Boise, provisioned there, and then started south for California on a course which proved unsatisfactory. Joseph Walker took the larger section of the company with all the wagons and made his way to the Humboldt River, probably along the Goose Creek route, which continued in use. The Humboldt was not new to Walker. Just ten years before, he had led a group of Captain Bonneville's trappers to California along the full length of the valley, and returned eastward, also, by following its course, fighting Indians both going and returning. The country was familiar to him, but even so he was not able to find a way for the 1843 wagons to cross the Sierra, and they were abandoned on the eastern slope.

Old Greenwood had no intention of failing to get his wagons through. Neither did he intend to quarrel with the Indians if a clash could be avoided. He could not speak the Shoshone tongue which was almost universal on the trail west of the Rockies, but he was adept with the sign language. The party journeyed down the long meager valley of the Humboldt without notable difficulty and stopped at or near the Great Meadows to plot out their next procedure.

They had been camped but a short time when an Indian arrived, with some dignity. He was a chief of the Pah Utes, and this was an official visit to find out what the white men were doing there and what were their purposes. With thorough knowledge of what was proper according to Indian etiquette, Old Greenwood went into a long-drawn-out discussion in sign language aided by diagrams drawn in the sand. Presently he accumulated the information that, fifty or sixty miles ahead, was a river which cut through the California Mountains, as the Sierra Nevada was then called. By following the canyon of that river, the chief stated, the white people could surmount the range.

Old Caleb thought that this route promised better than Joseph Walker's, and the leaders of the migration decided to put it to the test. The company remained camped while horsemen went ahead to see whether the river actually was there or the canny chief was misleading them. They came back affirming its presence. Therefore, as it was then the first of October and precariously late in the season, they chanced that the rest of the data was given in good faith and took the Indian's advice.

Apparently the eccentric chief liked the white people, and it is certain that they liked him. They at once dubbed him "Truckee." Some say that it was because he resembled a Canadian of that name whom some members of the party had known; others, that it was because he answered in his own language, "Truckee, Truckee," when he meant "all right." He did not ask for reasons but unquestionably adopted the appellation as his "white man's name." Looking ahead in history we find that he was the father of Winnemucca, chief in his turn of the Pah Utes.

The Murphy-Stevens-Townsend party called the lovely stream, which they ascended into California, Truckee's River. And in using its canyon as a thoroughfare Old Greenwood pioneered a route which has never been materially altered and is still followed by railroad and highway.

The wagons of 1844 stayed in the canyon until it opened into the meadows that surround the present town of Truckee; but it was (before modern engineering smoothed the way) difficult beyond all reason. The man who guided the wagons of the next migration, in 1845, decided that it would be easier to leave the canyon at what is now Verdi and go into the meadows by way of Dog Valley and Alder Creek (as they are now called). The wagons of 1845 and all subsequent migrations did so. We are indebted to the manuscript reminiscences of Thomas Knight for this information. He does not name the guide who instituted the change, but as Old Greenwood is known to have been hired as pilot for the migration of 1845, and as the guide mentioned in Knight's manuscript was evidently acquainted with the difficulties which the first wagons had in the canyon, it sounds remarkably as if Caleb had plotted out another permanent improvement in the trail. Particularly does this conclusion seem inescapable since Greenwood was the only available guide who was qualified to show the route; Joseph Walker, who might have made a successful try at it, being with Frémont that year. The data indicate that Old Greenwood should be credited with this achievement.

The pioneering families of 1844 emerged from Truckee Canyon with relief and plodded across the meadows. Here they could travel comfortably and with reasonable speed. Ahead, in plain sight, was the solid granite backbone of the Sierra and, notched between the peaks, the forbidding though gloriously beautiful pass known for many years as Truckee's Pass and nowadays called the Donner Summit.

The company moved west up the river a few miles, but presently, while still in the meadow, the stream curved to the south and continued in that direction some fourteen miles to its source in magnificent Lake Tahoe. Near the bend where it made its directional change was the junction with its little tributary, now called Donner Lake Creek. This creek is about two miles long and flows from Donner Lake, as it is now called. The 1844 company called it Truckee's Lake; it lay directly to the west between the curve of the river and the pass.

And right here a strange, almost unbelievable, thing happened. In this age of protected comfort we cannot even attempt to imagine the exigencies that forced the actions of these first travelers more than one hundred years ago. A mixed party was traveling ahead of the wagons—two women and four men. Apparently it was composed of the personnel of the company who just happened to be on horseback that day. They were Miss Ellen Murphy, Mrs. Townsend, who had been in frail health for a long time and was considered almost an invalid, her servant, Francis, John

Murphy, Daniel Murphy, and Oliver Magnan. When they came to the curve of the Truckee they paid no attention to its change of direction but continued along the bank. The wagons, coming up later under the direction of Old Caleb, were not deflected from their westward course and turned up Donner Lake Creek toward the crest of the Sierra. The two parties did not meet again until they reached Sutter's Fort in the Sacramento Valley, three weeks later.

The story has two versions. One is that the separation had been planned. The other, told by one of the horsemen in later years, is that no such plan had been agreed upon and that the wagons simply continued west without communicating with them. It well may have been that the weather was too threatening to permit delay of any kind. It would have been quite in character for Old Greenwood to advise that the strayed horseback party must make its way alone rather than jeopardize the whole company by time wasted in attempted consolidation.

Winter descended whitely upon the mountains. When the horse party ascended the east bank of the Truckee and thus became the first emigrants to see the blue glory of Lake Tahoe two feet of snow was upon the ground. They forded the icy river and scrambled over the mountains to the American River. It was running full and swollen; we therefore can be sure that the fresh fall of snow had begun to melt by that time. The men were good hunters, and the deer had not yet deserted the mountains. The party did not suffer for lack of food. Their worst hardship and danger was the continual crossing of the American River, which of course they could not avoid, since they had no knowledge of the cliffs and curves.

Twenty-one days from the time when they took the wrong turn on the Truckee River the little company of six reached Sinclair's rancho and, a couple of miles farther, Sutter's Fort.

In the meantime Old Greenwood and the rest of the company had camped at the east end of Truckee's Lake to decide what was to be done. Dr. John Townsend and his father-in-law, Schallenberger, had merchandise of value in their wagons. They looked at the apparently unscalable cliffs ahead and decided to leave their goods there for the winter. For guard duty during the long months Moses Schallenberger volunteered. He was still a growing boy, but courageous and self-reliant. Joseph Foster and Allen Montgomery then offered to remain with him.

The company left them two cows and went on. The three were quite cheerful about the experience. All the wagons had been left except five which were still with the main party. Game seemed plentiful. They could not know that the bear would hibernate and the deer leave for lower altitudes. They cut saplings, using the cows to haul them, and built a rude house, twelve by fourteen feet.

They expected that the snow would not exceed the two feet which had fallen and already partly melted. This, unfortunately, was wishful thinking. They also reasoned that the nude Indians would remain below the snow line and not interfere with them, which proved true as long as winter lasted.

After their cabin was complete they made beef of the cows and preserved it in the snow, which increased to a depth that completely engulfed the tiny building. Also, to their consternation, the game vanished. The supply of beef dwindled day by day, and nothing was killed to take its place.

The three decided that to stay would be suicide. They started for the Sacramento Valley and had reached the top of the pass when young Moses (only seventeen, poor lad) began to have severe cramps and to fall in the snow every little way. It was evident that he could not make the trip. He turned back, and the other two went on.

In telling the story to his daughters many years later Schallenberger stressed the point that there was no alternative. Foster and Montgomery would have gone back with him had it been best, but there was not enough beef for one, let alone three. They took their lives in their hands in going on; he sadly risked his in going back. They parted in grief, not knowing whether they would ever see one another again.

The story of Moses Schallenberger is an epic in itself. He managed to regain the shelter of the cabin, recuperated for a few days, and settled down to outlast the winter. Among the baggage he found traps and set them. At first he caught a coyote, which, presenting itself to be eaten when he had been accustomed to beef, nauseated the boy and filled him with such loathing that he could scarcely speak of it in later years. Afterward he caught foxes that seemed, by comparison, almost appetizing. He found Dr. Townsend's books and read aloud to himself for company. When, in the spring, the company sent back for him, he was in very fair condition—all things considered.

Beyond Truckee's Lake, Old Greenwood, the rest of the company, and five wagons faced the granite cliffs of the summit. They had traveled along the north side of the lake and, as members of the party afterward stated, surmounted the crest of the range in the pass later used by the railroad.

Edwin Bryant, in his 1846 journal called *What I Saw in California,* gives the first description written on the spot:

Standing at the bottom [he wrote] and looking upwards at the perpendicular, and in some places, impending granite cliffs, the observer, without any further knowledge on the subject, would doubt if man or beast ever made good a passage over them. But we knew that man and horse, oxen and wagon, women and children, had crossed this formidable and apparently impassable barrier erected by Nature between the desert and the fertile districts on the coast of the Pacific. What their energy had accomplished, impelled though it had been by an invincible desperation, we knew could be achieved by us.

And he did achieve it; but Bryant led a pack train. Greenwood's problem was increased a hundredfold by wagons and the fact that no one had preceded him to show him where he might avoid a dead end and the retracing of his route. In one place there was a sheer wall of rock; it looked like an impasse. But a narrow cleft through the granite would admit the passage of one ox at a time. The willing animals were unyoked and led through the gap, scrambling upward to the top of the rock wall where, with chains, they were able to pull the empty wagons straight up the face of the perpendicular granite. The party reassembled the baggage at the top and went on.

The summit was the end of the struggle. The downgrade was slight. Bryant wrote, "A mile brought us to a small dimple on the top of the mountain, in the center of which is a miniature lake, surrounded by green grass." This is now called Mary's Lake.

The forty-niners varied this route by ascending to the crest of the mountains up Coldstream, the next canyon to the south. The divergence occurred east of Truckee's Lake; the gold seekers did not see its waters at all unless they took a detour of less than a mile through the trees for the purpose. The pass they used lay between Mount Judah and its next neighbor to the south, Mount Lincoln. The forty-niners rejoined the original trail in Summit Valley.

For years there has been a friendly difference of opinion among authorities over the date when the Coldstream road replaced the original trail. Through a series of happy findings among the manuscripts of various libraries we have been able to come within a week or two of the precise date: Bryant's journal tells us that when he made the ascent on August 25, 1846, the trail still went north of Truckee's Lake and through the pass where the railroad now is. The diary of Nicholas Carriger, taken in combination with information contained in his later reminiscences and the 1849 diary of D. Jagger, informs the reader that, on September 21, 1846, the Carriger company constructed a windlass at the summit of Coldstream Canyon. The idea was conceived by a Mr. Judson Green, one of the party, and approved by their pilot, Mr. Greenwood. Carriger does not specify which canyon they used, but Jagger wrote on August 22, 1849: "At the summit we collected a quantity of snow which had made us a delicious drink today. At the same place we saw the windlass with which the first emigrants to California drew up their wagons." Jagger's notations show that he took the regular '49 trail up Coldstream. Knowing that Old Greenwood installed the windlass for the first party known to have traveled the Coldstream Canyon, and considering his tendency to find a new route if he did not like the old one, we may take him as the likeliest possibility for the pathfinder, and September 21, 1846, as the likeliest date for the opening of the Coldstream trail. True, he started out in that year as guide for the Aram party, but he separated from them near the Sink of the Humboldt, and Chief Truckee was persuaded to travel to California as their guide. The little-read documents by Carriger give interesting information about what the strong-minded octogenarian did during the rest of the journey to the Sacramento Valley.

It may be added that (as far as we know) no wagon party used the railroad pass after September 21, and no party went up Coldstream before that date. Mary Jones stated in her 1846 reminiscences that her group made use of the windlass. Heinrich Lienhard, on October 4, must have gone up Coldstream, since he did not see Truckee's Lake. James Frazier Reed's hand-drawn map shows that he took the Coldstream route at the end of the second week in October, 1846. And W. C. Graves, a survivor of the Donner party, told C. F. McGlashan that when that company arrived—the last of all the emigrants of the year—the emigrant road "followed up Coldstream, and so crossed the dividing ridge."

There are some gaps in this proof, but the presumption is strong that Old Greenwood is the one who deserves credit for opening the Coldstream route.

To return to 1844 and the maiden journey of wagons over the Sierra: From Mary's Lake they dropped gently into what was later called Summit Valley and is now largely occupied by the waters of artificial Lake Van Orden. From there they followed the course of Yuba River through difficulties almost unimaginable. No simpler route was found, and the gold seekers cursed the rocky canyon throughout the entire gold rush. One of the worst places, the granite slide mentioned by Bryarly, is on the precipitous downslope near the Rainbow Tavern. The Yuba was forded just a short distance below. The forty-niners said that had they not known that wagons had gone ahead of them they could not have believed that the passage was possible.

Old Greenwood watched the first snow fly and decided that they must travel faster, yet he was bound to save the wagons. His reasoning was simple and direct. The women, the children, and the wagons hindered progress; therefore they would leave the women, the children, and the wagons and come back for them next spring. And they did just that. Furthermore, it was a successful policy. In the end they came through without loss of life.

They built two cabins (or, more probably, a cabin with a lean-to) near the great spring which is one of the headwaters of the Yuba. This was the best description that the men could give when asked in later years. They also figured that they had gone about twenty miles beyond the summit. The only great spring reasonably near that distance is Crystal Springs— now dammed and known as Crystal Lake. It lies at the top of a steep pull out from Yuba River and close to Cisco Butte. The cabins were probably built in the tree-sheltered hollow below, between the spring and the river. Three travelers, not of the original party, are known to have seen the cabins: James Frazier Reed, in October, 1846, marked "cabins" on his map at approximately this spot. Markle and Bryarly saw the burnt remains of the cabins in 1849, after they had come down the granite slide near Rainbow Tavern and before reaching Bear Valley.

Near the only great spring in that distance the trail breakers of 1844 left their women—four of them, with at least ten children—under the protection of the husband of one of their number and an old man. Here, early in the year 1845, Elizabeth Murphy was born. She was probably the first girl born to American overland emigrants in California, but must yield to Adelaide, the short-lived little daughter of Thomas O. Larkin, American consul at Monterey, the honor of being the first American girl born in California.

The men of the party moved on at an accelerated pace. With superlative woodcraft, Caleb took them through Bear Valley and over the ridges of the foothills to emerge into the Sacramento Valley near what is now Wheatland. And so the '49 trail by way of Truckee Pass evolved, and it continued in use as long as an overland trail was needed.

These men arrived at Sutter's Fort almost coincidentally with the horse party that had come down the American River. Finding the country torn by dissensions and in the process of overthrowing the Mexican governor, Micheltorena, they took John Sutter's word for the right of the case and decided to spend the winter fighting for Mexico, to make their new home safe. This they proceeded to do, marching as far south as Santa Barbara. But when spring began to show in the mountains, the men of the '44 migration quit the cause cold and marched back to get their women. The five wagons left at the women's camp were brought on—the first to arrive overland in the Sacramento Valley. The ones left east of the summit could not be hauled over so soon, but Dennis Martin courageously made the trek over the mountain tops to get Moses Schallenberger, and the two arrived in the valley at the same time as the women. Before the unguarded wagons at Truckee's Lake could be salvaged, the Indians had completely despoiled them.

To Old Greenwood belongs the distinction of having guided the party that opened the main overland trail through Truckee Pass, later called the Gold Trail. To this honor we can add the suspicion, amounting to a moral certainty, that he also pioneered its two main variants: the Dog Valley–Alder Creek route and the Coldstream trail. He opened the way to California and is worthy to be classed with Joseph Walker and Jedediah Smith as a pathfinder of the first water.

BIBLIOGRAPHY

BRYANT, EDWIN. *What I Saw in California: Being the Journal of a Tour by the Emigrant Route and South Pass ... 1846–1847.* New York, 1848.

CARRIGER, NICHOLAS. Journal Crossing the Plains to California in 1846. MS, Bancroft Library, University of California.

————. Autobiography [including a short narrative of the same trip, written in 1874]. MS No. 6, in Sketches of Californian Pioneers, Bancroft Library.

GEIGER, VINCENT, and WAKEMAN BRYARLY. *Trail to California: The Overland Journal of Vincent Geiger and Wakeman Bryarly.* Edited by David M. Potter. New Haven, 1945.

JAGGER, D. Diary written on the emigrant trail in 1849. MS in Templeton Crocker Collection, California Historical Society Library, San Francisco.

JONES, MARY A. Recollections of 1846. Compiled by Mrs. J. C. Jones, Alamo, California. Typescript, Bancroft Library

KNIGHT, THOMAS. Recollections [of 1845, written in 1872]. MS No. 18 in Sketches of Californian Pioneers, Bancroft Library.

LIENHARD, HEINRICH. Heinrich Lienhard in California, 1846–1850. Translation from the German original by Reuben Louis Spaeth. MS, M.A. thesis, University of California Library.

MARKLE, JOHN A. The Travell of a Gold Digger, enroute California, 1849. Photostat of MS, Bancroft Library; original in the possession of Auburn Parlor of Native Sons of the Golden West, Auburn, California.

McGLASHAN, C. F. *History of the Donner Party.* Truckee, California, 1879.

REED, JAMES FRAZIER. Hand-drawn map of a portion of the Humboldt River and the Sierra Nevada, showing emigrant trail and camp sites. Captions in handwriting of Reed and bearing the date October 13, 1846. Sutter's Fort, Sacramento, California.

The Outfitting Posts

WALKER D. WYMAN

[Walker D. Wyman is chairman of the department of social sciences in the River Falls, Wisconsin, State Teachers College. To the California Historical Society *Quarterly* in 1945 he contributed four installments of "California Emigrant Letters," collected from their first printing in various midwestern newspapers.]

WHEN THE NEWS of the gold discoveries in California filtered back to the "States" in the late summer of 1848 a considerable number of people were thrilled at the prospect of abolishing poverty from their particular world by going overland or by sea to that Utopia on the Pacific. One man spoke for many when he said: " 'I believe I'll go. I know most of this talk is wildly exaggerated, but I am sensible enough to discount it and to disbelieve absurd stories. . . . In fact, if I don't pick up more than a hatful of gold a day I shall be perfectly satisfied.' "[1] The news came too late for people of the Mississippi Valley and the Atlantic Coast to emigrate that fall, but it came in time to allow a good deal of planning to be done around the firesides and cracker barrels that winter. For those living outside the Mississippi Valley it seemed practicable to go by sea, round Cape Horn, or mostly by sea, crossing the Isthmus of Panama or some other narrow part of the continent. But to the great group of hopefuls living along the outstretched arms of the Mississippi River the way to Eldorado was by overland trail, and especially by the central overland route up the Platte River.

For many years the political frontier had been the Rocky Mountains, except in the Pacific Northwest where the United States shared claims with other powers. By the time of the gold rush the westward movement, long poised on a geographic dead center on the edge of the Great Plains and Indian country, had begun to skip great distances. Already Americans were in Texas, Utah, Oregon, California, and New Mexico. Already the mountain men, explorers, and emigrants had found the great trails leading to the Transmontane West. The central overland route was well traced by those foot-loose Americans whom Edmund Burke once feared would become the nomads and the Cossacks of the English-speaking frontier. Up the Platte had gone the Mormons, Oregonians, and early emigrants to California, and from these emigrations had come not only a broader trail but knowledge of travel to many accustomed to living in

---

[1] Quoted in Stewart Edward White, *The Forty-Niners* (New Haven, 1918), 64.

[14]

an environment of forest or prairie with plenty of rainfall. Already there had risen on the Missouri River frontier three settlements from which emigrants departed for the West. These were to become the important outfitting posts of the California trek.

Prior to 1849 the overland emigrants were mainly farmers from areas adjacent to the Missouri frontier. If they were bound for Salt Lake or Oregon they went in their own wagons pulled by their own oxen, and from their own larders they supplied the dried foods, preserved meat, and other products necessary for the long trip through a country generally devoid of white settlements. The forty-niners caused a new set of circumstances to appear. Here was a polyglot people, many of whom were fresh from urban centers and ignorant of frontier travel. Many lacked not only calluses on their hands but also knowledge of cookery, the handling of animals, repairing of wagons, fording of rivers, and other aspects of travel. Argonaut farmers generally organized into groups in their own community, outfitted themselves, and struck for the closest ferry on the Missouri River. But the thousands of others boarded the steamboats and were deposited at one of the three settlements, and there they made their purchases, acquired much of their information about travel, and organized into companies for mutual protection in a land without law. It was this economic and social need, as well as the requirement of a ferry to cross the river (except at Independence), that made Independence and St. Joseph in Missouri and Kanesville in Iowa outposts of importance in the gold rush of 1849–1850. At these little towns, in each of those years, from 20,000 to 30,000 persons gathered to go overland to California.[2]

Since the business of outfitting was in its infancy in 1849 it is remarkable that the emigrants found sufficient supplies of wagons, animals, foodstuffs, and mining equipment for sale. The farm areas in the immediate hinterland produced surpluses, but these had to be supplemented by products from miles behind the frontier. Great herds of oxen, wagons from St. Louis and farther east, flour from the mills of a wide area, all met the emergency in the spring months of the years of the great emigration. The steamboat with its supplies, the drovers, the merchants, and the informal middlemen who sold in the streets all became cogs in the busy wheel of the outfitting business. With this business came not only prosperity for the outfitters but also dreams of a golden future, that of digging gold in a Missouri outpost rather than going to California for it.

---

[2] Probably more than thirty thousand in 1850.

Here, then, where the Missouri connected with the trails to the West, was the intermediary point in the trek to the Sacramento Valley. It was the place where the emigrant probably had his first taste of camp life, where weeks spent in getting ready saw busy men doing their own cooking, washing clothes, and puttering around getting everything properly placed in the wagons. Here the traveler wrote what he thought to be his last letter home, spent much time organizing a congenial group, and probably visited most of the taverns. Some even lost their stakes to card-sharps and faced the humiliation of going home rather than west. Others decided to go home anyway, and more turned back after the first reverses on the plains. But as the grass came up bright and green on the prairies west of the river it was time to go, and for weeks the inadequate ferries carried them over. The town by June was as quiet as a cemetery and nearly as dead. The flood was over; only the permanent improvements and the debris remained.

INDEPENDENCE

Independence was the oldest and the best known of the Missouri River towns in 1849. Situated four miles below the river and ten miles east of the state boundary where the river makes its great bend, it had long been known as a terminus of the Santa Fe Trail, which extended eight hundred miles into the Southwest. Since its founding in 1827 the settlement had lived on the "truck and dicker" trade with the local Indians, the fur traders, and the bullwhackers. From it in the early 'eighteen-forties the first emigrants had departed for Oregon and a few had gone to California. By 1849 its primacy as a point of departure for the Oregon and California emigrants was being seriously threatened by St. Joseph, a few miles north on the river. In the year of the great avalanche it claimed a population of 1,600, thirty stores, two "large and fine hotels," numerous boarding houses, and twenty blacksmith shops. Here, in the minds of the residents, was a town made to order for the prospective Californians: merchants knew the outfitting business from experience; wagonmakers knew the art of manufacturing vehicles that would stand up under the travel of the arid plains; farmers were numerous enough to produce foodstuffs and work animals to meet all the needs. Indeed, the Missouri mule, whose progenitors had come up the Santa Fe Trail from the Spanish Southwest, was there in numbers. If these people could not outfit an Argonaut, who could? asked the vocal element of that town.[3]

[3] The information on Independence and the other river towns comes principally from their weekly newspapers, the St. Louis *Missouri Republican*, *Niles' National Register*, and published diaries.

Local merchants were cheered when the New York *Tribune* recommended to its readers an early start by way of Independence and the Santa Fe Trail; but this endorsement was blunted by the failure of two St. Louis papers to give preference to the town. The correspondent of one of them even ridiculed the wagons made in Independence. "More than once," he wrote, "have I seen wagons lying with the wheel crushed on the road between my lodgings and the town." To offset these criticisms the town fathers issued handbills and distributed them to emigrants on the steamboats coming up the river from St. Louis.

Despite these difficulties, emigrants did come, not by the hundreds but by the thousands. Even a newspaper of St. Joseph, the rival upstream, admitted that between six thousand and eight thousand people left Independence for the mines. In these spring months the scenes around this little outpost must have been exciting for everybody. Hundreds of wagons were encamped there almost any time between late March and June. The streets were thronged with bearded men, and it seemed that nearly everyone carried a gun and had a Bowie knife in his belt. There was one lone soul who, with his rifle on his shoulder and a bulldog at his heel, had walked all the way from Maine and planned to walk the rest of the distance to California. To one who mixed with this heterogeneous group it seemed that everybody was "in a hurry, jostling one another and impatient to get through their business. Mules and oxen strove for the right of way, while the loud cracking of ox goads, squeaking of wheels and rattling of chains, mingled with the oaths of the teamsters, produced a din indescribable."[4] In the evenings some sat around their campfires writing letters home or playing cards; others gathered in the saloons, where some quarreled, fought, gambled, and otherwise passed the time away. It was reported in early April that a number had "attempted to whip the 'tiger' but instead have been fleeced of their all . . ." and were on the way home instead of to California.[5]

The supply of mules and oxen was apparently greater than the demand in the 1849 rush, but many were of low quality. Prices ranged from $22 to $65 per yoke of oxen, and from $30 to $100 a head for either Spanish or American mules. The inexperienced traveler who bought wild young

[4] From the diary of W. G. Johnston, in Valeski Bari, ed., *The Course of Empire* (New York, 1931), 75–76.

[5] This letter, written from the emigrant camps by a correspondent, appeared in the *Missouri Republican*, April 10, 1849. For other letters written by emigrants in the Missouri River towns, at or en route to the mines, see those compiled by the writer and published in the issues, March through December, 1945, of the California Historical Society *Quarterly*.

animals must have provided considerable entertainment to old hands when the breaking period began. One wrote thus of such a day's work:

> We tried our skill today at breaking mules, but having heretofore had no experience or acquaintance with the long-eared animals, we found it to be a more difficult task than we had supposed. . . . They were young mules which had never been halter-broken, and were about as wild as the deer on the prairie. A wild, unbroken mule is the most desperate animal that I have ever seen. . . . They would kick, bite and strike with their fore feet, making it very dangerous to go about them.[6]

Cholera appeared in the emigrant camps early in May and encouraged hasty departure from town. Thirty-four deaths were reported in one week, principally among the Californians. Within two weeks the cholera had run its course and so had the emigration. Never again were so many gold seekers to thrill this little river town. In 1850 the two other settlements above it were to take over much of this business, leaving undisturbed the Santa Fe trade centered there for the time. Independence had its golden hour in the spring months of 1849.

St. Joseph

Fortunate it was for the emigrants of 1849–1850 that there was more than one place on the Missouri where they could come by steamboat and prepare for the overland trip. Independence would have been unable to accommodate the thousands who left the Missouri River frontier for California in 1849 and 1850. St. Joseph, situated north of the great bend and therefore eighty miles closer to the Platte River trail, became the leading outfitting place in the California movement.

In the year of the Louisiana Purchase there was "quite a stir" among the Indians of the "Black Snake Hills" area when the first fur post was established there by Joseph Robidoux. In the subsequent years the hinterland filled in with farmers, the town was platted, and, in the early 'forties when the Oregon movement began, some emigrants crossed the river at "St. Jo." By 1849 this settlement claimed more than fifteen hundred inhabitants, eighteen stores, two pork-packing establishments, two steam sawmills, two flour mills, two "mechanic shops," three churches, two newspapers, several saloons, a courthouse, and a triweekly stage, and it produced surpluses that were sent down the river to St. Louis in the three steamboats that stuck their prows in the mudbanks at the levee. The merchants had been outfitting a greater number of California and

---

[6] Kimball Webster, *The Gold Seekers of '49* (Manchester, New Hampshire, 1917), 34–35.

Oregon emigrants than Independence for several years, and no doubt they were quite aware of the demands of the travel. In the weekly *Adventure* in March, 1848, appeared an advertisement directed only to Far West emigrants, apparently the first such advertising on the frontier.

OREGON AND CALIFORNIA
NEW AND CHEAP
CASH STORE

... We would especially call attention of Oregon and California emigrants to our stock of goods, a large proportion of which has been purchased for that particular trade; and we flatter ourselves that we can furnish the same as low as they can be had in the West. Brown drills, Osnaburgs, blue drills, and camp kettles, tin plates, powder, lead, etc., etc., can be had at very low prices. ...

In the winter of 1848–1849 eastern innocents began to make inquiry as to routes, needs, and prices, and this gave the papers the opportunity to advance arguments favorable to St. Joseph as a starting place. The "case" ran thus: easily accessible by water and land; cheaper prices than at Independence; patronage of the California and Oregon emigrants over the years; closer to San Francisco than Independence; abundance of supplies for overland travel.

Steamboats began to dump their human cargo at St. Joseph long before the warm weather arrived. Here they either gave in to the hotel "runners," went to a boarding house, purchased camping equipment, and started learning what all of them had to learn sooner or later, or else made an arrangement to join a group that was already formed. Companies arriving already equipped crossed the river by ferry and encamped while waiting for the grass to grow and they tested the adequacy of their provisions. Long lines of wagons daily filed through town to wait for their turns to cross, while those still in the process impatiently counted the mouths that would eat the grass or the number of pick-axes that would strike great veins of gold ahead of them. In town, churches and lodges were crowded and the streets and taverns were the scenes of many fights and brawls. One Missourian en route to the mines wrote: "Eastern men particularly are sadly out of fix here, and we have almost calculable advantage over them in fixing up for the trip. And the Missourians are skinning them most horribly too, in everything they purchase ..." Another wrote of the scenes in town early in May:

The streets of this fine little town of St. Joseph were in a complete jam ... We had the noise of the steamboats, the confusion of voices, the looing of cows ... the unmusical noise of the organ-grinding girls, with all sorts of accompaniments, also the musical noise of the mules—a lot of which were on sale at a street corner—and among this mass there was but one that had had a "drop too much," and he was not bound for Californy, but St. Louey; he wasn't one of them as was going to starve on the plains and be eat by wolves, but he was going to St. Louey whar whisky was plenty

Joseph Robidoux's ferry was no longer adequate to bridge the river at this point. Four now were in operation, two of which were several miles above town. They were four or five days behind schedule though they were taking across 150 wagons each day and the steamboats on occasion served as ferries for a consideration of $5.00 to $10.00 a wagon. By the middle of May, 2,850 wagons had paid ferriage at St. Joseph, while another 1,500 had crossed above the town.

Cholera visited the emigrants there in April. Although only seven deaths were reported, the companies hastened their organization and departure, for it was commonly but mistakenly believed that the disease would not follow them to the plains.

Robidoux's town on the hills had reason to feel that it had either been favored or mauled by the emigration of 1849, since close to half of the entire overland emigration up the Platte had crossed the river and outfitted in whole or in part there. The effect upon the town was salutary. The gold seekers of 1850, who came in greater numbers than in 1849, found a population of three thousand, with four hotels, twenty-six stores, twelve blacksmith shops, six or eight wagonmakers' establishments, and several warehouses and bakeries. Since the mercantile interests did not expect quite the windfall in 1850 that they had in 1849 (and this remains one of the amazing aspects of the California gold rush), they were not adequately prepared for the outfitting demands. The local newspaper estimated that thirty thousand people had left for the plains from "Blacksnake Hills," and even though this figure is probably too high, it does explain why some articles were scarce and dear long before the customers had left the busy streets and business houses. One man bound for riches wrote home advising emigrants to "take everything along with them that they can, as every little thing costs three or four times as much as it does at home. The markets are filled with broken-down horses jockeyed up for the occasion, and unbroken mules which they assure you are as handy as sheep. . . ." The growing city, though it had by now acquired a reputation for harboring various thieves and confidence men and as a place where a man "had to guard his horse as if he were in Indian Territory," had enabled thousands of Californians to start West. It deserves a greater reputation than it has as an important bead on the economic rosary that was the Missouri River in the days of the great emigration to California.

KANESVILLE

In the gold rush of 1849 and 1850 the area around the mouth of the Platte River made no great contribution to the emigrants who came to the frontier by steamboat. Hundreds did cross the river here, but they were for the most part those who had come equipped from farm and town back across the prairies of Iowa. There was no town then that could exclusively claim the name of Council Bluffs. The name may have been applied originally to the bluffs where Lewis and Clark held an Indian council in 1804. It is certain that the Omaha Indian agency shared the name in 1849, since it is known that some emigrants did get mail there addressed to Council Bluffs. The subagency for the Indians on the Iowa side of the river also shared the name. Anyway, what is today Council Bluffs, Iowa, was not then in existence as such, but the Mormon settlement of Kanesville was, and it, the future Council Bluffs, was the only settlement that had ambitions to sell to emigrants.

Just why Kanesville had outfitting dreams is difficult to understand. It was only two years old when the avalanche moved toward California, being a Saints' frontier outpost to be held and occupied only until they could be moved to the Salt Lake Valley. The winter of 1848–1849 had been severe, and most of their surplus crops had been consumed by the livestock. The major factors in favor of emigrants' using such a place were the geographic fact that Kanesville did stand at the head of the Mormon Trail up the north side of the Platte and the presence in the town of a number of people who were familiar with frontier travel. While at least sixteen steamboats did bring Californians there in 1849, and at least five hundred wagons did cross below the mouth of the Platte, the evaluation of the town given by one traveler was perhaps correct:

I found Kanesville to be a very dirty, unhealthy place, and withal a very dear place to... outfit for the Plains, notwithstanding the assertions of holders of property and merchants ... there to the contrary. They assure emigrants that their wisest plan is to take their money there to purchase their outfit, but I hope few will believe them, for as there is not much competition they get prices the very reverse of their consciences. . . .[7]

The few who did come in 1849 did gain information from the residents on the conditions of travel up the Platte; some did visit the shop of the

---

[7] James Linforth, *Route from Liverpool to Great Salt Lake Valley* (London, 1855), 79; also quoted by Alfred Sorenson in *The Story of Omaha* ... (Omaha, 1923), 26.

Browning "revolving rifle" and saw a gun that was to evolve into a famous weapon of war; some did visit the grogshop near the tabernacle, called by the faithful, "a low miserable sink—a place of drunkenness and gambling on the Sabbath-day, where men get so filled with whiskey that they blaspheme everything that is good. . . ." All formed companies with such names as "Missouri and Iowa Mining Company," "Mutual Protection Company," "Iowa and Wisconsin Mining Company," "The Extract Company," "Union Packing Company," "California Banner Company," and the "Social Bank of Liberty." Auctions were often held in the streets by those who decided to stay in Kanesville. One reported seeing an "infatuated lover of bargains, who, although he had but one wagon and a sick wife, who would be certain to occupy it always, was silly enough to attend these auctions and buy up 'bargains' enough to stock a London 'bottle-wop shop.' Gambling houses and lawyers abound also. Where there are so many wolves there must . . . be a number of victims."[8]

After the first year's gold rush Kanesville was a sedate little settlement of five hundred, gradually being converted from a Mormon to a Gentile town. Had there been no gold rush through it in 1850 and in subsequent years, it is doubtful whether the church officers would have had any great trouble in getting the Saints to move "home." The outfitting business caused the economic adrenalin to flow, and in the days of frontier poverty this was welcome to all and sundry. Orson Hyde, the Mormon leader of western Iowa, sought to focus the emigration there. He assured the readers of the *Frontier Guardian* in twelve states that the local merchants (and there were thirteen stores and two hotels in the spring of 1850) were preparing to care for the emigrants' needs in the second year of the gold rush. He further recommended as a desirable speculation that cows and steers be driven from the Mississippi River to Kanesville. The North Platte route was known to be, said he, the "shortest, safest, healthiest, and altogether the best route . . ." to the West. This was said at a time when the church had decided to send its faithful to Salt Lake on the route below the Platte.

By April Fools' Day Californians were in town in numbers. Hyde advised his readers to accommodate them with shelter and to sell reasonably to them. "They are strangers among us. Make them as comfortable as you can, and remember that we have been strangers in strange lands." By May the number of adventurers was greater than even the optimistic had anticipated, and Kanesville was like a drowning man going down

---

[8] Sorenson, *op. cit.*, 26.

for the third time. Most of the pilgrims seem to have been wagon emigrants from the East, for only twelve steamboats had brought their human cargoes up by the latter part of May. It was estimated that between four thousand and five thousand wagons had passed through the "holler." This seems high for Kanesville, where there was not even a ferry, but certainly not too high for the Council Bluffs area which was served by four ferries—three some distance below town and one twelve miles above at Winter Quarters. At least enough emigrants came to deplete the available supplies, causing merchants to send downstream for more goods. At the end of the season the population had grown to one thousand and the number of stores to nineteen. Five steamboats were then making more or less regular trips up from St. Louis. Local officials complained of the returning gold seekers and the Gentiles who had settled down there as being demoralizing influences in the community, and it was asserted that there were some "scaly" people among the emigrants. Kanesville in transition then continued as an outpost, and in 1853, seeking to capitalize on the reputation of the Council Bluffs area, officially changed the name to Council Bluffs. This was regarded as downright knavery by competing towns but as an important move by those looking toward an outfitting future.

Albert Richardson once wrote that man "can no more focus the emigration's converging rays than he can by taking thought add one cubit to his stature." The three Missouri River outposts in the period of the great California exodus never believed this to be true. It was that focusing of the emigration that they hoped to accomplish. Geography largely determined the place to which an Argonaut would go to cross the river if he were already equipped. But the reputation of the outfitting town determined in no small degree the place to which a pilgrim would buy his steamboat ticket. Independence capitalized on its early reputation as a Santa Fe Trail terminus and as a starting place for the first Oregonians, but it had to surrender its primacy to St. Joseph, higher on the river, which also had a favorable reputation among the pre-1849 emigrants. Kanesville was too high on the river for the majority of the steamboat emigrants, and as a consequence, despite its Mormon experience, outfitted fewer than did the two lower towns. Advertising by the commercial interests was limited principally to the distribution of the weekly paper and handbills. The river, the plains, and the reputation of the central overland trail—these were the principal factors focusing the human tide at these little posts on the Missouri River frontier.

From Louisiana to Mariposa

Edited by ROBERT GLASS CLELAND

[Robert Glass Cleland is a member of the permanent research staff at the Huntington Library. He is the author of numerous works in the field of California history; most recently, *The Cattle on a Thousand Hills* (San Marino, 1941), *From Wilderness to Empire* (New York, 1944), and *California in Our Time* (New York, 1948).]

JOSEPH POWNALL was a native of Hackettstown, New Jersey, and a graduate of the Medical Department of the University of the City of New York. Apparently a rover at heart, he practiced his profession first in Georgia, six months later in Florida, then, after a short interlude with the American forces at Matamoros and Monterrey, in New Orleans, and finally in De Soto Parish, Louisiana. In 1849 he joined the mass migration to California. There, after trying his fortunes in various places, he became a person of some distinction in the town of Columbia and one of the stockholders of the Tuolumne Water Company.

Like hundreds of his fellow Argonauts, Pownall kept a journal of his trip across the continent; and though he did not write as naturalist, physician, or man of letters, his account is interesting because of its descriptions of the route, the company's adventures and experiences, and the writer's own reactions to his environment. Pownall's journal and many of his letters came to the Huntington Library through the generous coöperation of Edwin Grabhorn of San Francisco.

Pownall's diary begins: "March 28th 1849 was an eventful day in Keachie Louisiana as many men stricken with the gold fever from Shreveport and nearby vicinities arrived here forming a company to get to California or bust." The diary ends at "Mariposa Diggings," September 7, 1849, with a note of reservation: "We bid adieu for a season to pack mules, pack saddles etc. but in exchange therefore I fear we take upon our selves a still more onerous burden, that of crowbar, spade and pick."

In the twenty-three weeks, more or less, that intervened between March 28 and September 7, Pownall and his companions crossed the entire state of Texas, turned south at El Paso into Chihuahua, presumably to avoid the Apache Indians, crossed into Sonora by way of the Guadalupe Pass, followed the long, dry trail through the future Gadsden Purchase territory to the Gila River, and rode down the Gila to the Colorado. After Pownall forded the Colorado at Yuma, he crossed the desert to Warner's

Ranch, when the summer heat was at its worst, and reached the picturesque but lawless pueblo of Los Angeles without further misadventure. From Los Angeles the company's route lay through Ventura, Santa Barbara, and San Luis Obispo to San Jose. There the members of the party went their several ways, and Pownall, with ten companions, found his way to the Mariposa diggings.

There were 51 members in the original company that left Keachie, Louisiana. At Dallas, Pownall and his associates joined forces with 56 other California-bound emigrants, and the party of 107 men was then divided into two companies, A and B. Before leaving Dallas, certain responsible members of the expedition drafted articles of government and conduct for the men to vote upon, but a number of would-be leaders raised "quibbling objections . . . which acted as yeast," and soon most of the hundred-odd members of the two companies were yelling and whooping "in glorious confusion."

Limitations of space make it necessary to omit the part of the diary that describes the journey from Louisiana to El Paso. Pownall speaks of friction within the company, a crisis precipitated by the desertion of the guide, and acute suffering caused by lack of water on this section of the route.

The expedition reached Socorro, New Mexico, on June 3, and went into camp for a week to give the livestock an opportunity to recuperate. Here two of the emigrants, Walter Beard and Byron B. Lee, quarreled over a kettle of beans, or some other trivial matter. Beard was the aggressor, but Lee, the smaller of the two men, had a knife in his hand when the fight started and stabbed Beard in three places, so that he died the next day. The other members of the company apparently ignored the incident.

We begin the diary with the crossing of the Rio Grande. Only trivial and obvious errors have been corrected in the text.

⚘ ⚘ ⚘

On *Sunday June 10th* the principal portion of our Company Crossed the Rio Grande opposite El Paso. I was behind & did not get over until the next day. *El Paso del Norte* is, as I suppose you may be aware, near the boundary line between Mexico & the U S. within *6 miles* of the *N E corner* of the *Mexican dominions*. It is a pleasant little Town containing with its environs about *8* or *10000* inhabitants[1] and so completely hidden

---

[1] El Paso del Norte, now Ciudad Juárez, Mexico, had about 1,000 inhabitants in 1849.

by shrubbery & trees that the traveler is in town before he is able to see it.
The houses are as is usual in North Mexico principally one story with
flat roof and built of adobes, that is large sun dried bricks. A *good deal*
of *attention* is paid to the *culture* of the *grape* & *large vineyards* are scattered in every direction indicating that it is a lucrative employment. I
here traded off my mare for a mule. I injured her withers some three
weeks before and in spite of all my efforts to cure, they were continually
getting worse. Had not this accident happened I should have kept her
for I was much attached to her. She might have carried me through.
If so, however, it would have been with about the same facility that a
certain miller of old named Jake Schneider managed to get into heaven
and that was by a *"tam tight squeeze."* We here obtained our *passports*
to travel in mexico and camped *7 miles* below on account of grass. While
here *3 mules* belonging to the Company were *stolen* and some of the company much exaspirated went back in search of them. Two of them being
a good deal under the influence of liquor concluded they had found the
thief & because he would not stop & be taken by them, fired on him
the whole contents of a revolver then went to the Alcalde or Prefect &
Swore vengeance on him unless the mules were given up. After *stamped-
ing* the whole place they *rode leisurely* back to camp. While they were
relating the story of their adventures an *expressman* from the *American
Consul* placed a letter in the hands of the Captn Stating that the whole
town was in confusion, that the bugle and drum were sounding the alarm
through every street, that the militia were hastening rapidly to their
quarters anxiously awaiting a hurried order to march &c. We took the
hint and packed up immediately if not sooner and vamosed. We afterwards learned that the man shot died that evening and that the drummer
was also shot. An account of it may have been published in some of the
U.S. papers if so, the above will explain the cause. Our next point of
destination was *Corralitos 160* miles distant, also in the State of Chihuahua and here I will jump in a car on the lightning line, for it is a barren
region having nothing to interest the traveller except the *Silver Mine 24
miles* from *Corallitos,* the proximity to which gives this town the only
importance it possesses.[2] We left here on the *20th* day *of June* and on

---

[2] Pownall and his companions followed a well-known trail which roughly paralleled the
present route of the Mexican Northwestern Railroad (Rio Grande, Sierra Madre, and Pacific
Railroad Branch) from El Paso to Corralitos. At Corralitos this trail joined the main route
from Chihuahua to California. See Ralph P. Bieber, ed., *Southern Trails to California in
1849* (Glendale, 1937), end map.

Corralitos was an Apache-ridden frontier town of three or four hundred people. The silver

the next day arrived at *Yanos*.[3] This place as well as Corralitos is kept in continual fear and suspense by the Apaches who infest the whole region of country from El Paso to the river Gila and frequently levy contributions by raids upon this or that town, hacienda or ranch as their savage fancies may consider more feasible or politic. Some *400* miles intervene between this *last* town & the *Rio Gila,* and one or two incidents only will I notice. On the next day after leaving Yanos, I *with some 15* others being 3 or 4 miles in advance came to the camping place and stopped. In a few minutes we noticed on the Slope of a hill near, 2 or 3 persons ascending, but as it was near the road we had just passed we concluded they were some of the company going up for the purpose of taking a view. The cry of "the Apaches are surrounding us" soon however placed us all on the qui vive and a small brush sure enough seemed inevitable. The arranging of packs, Staking of Animals and gathering up of guns was but the work of a moment and we stood ready to receive them. We then noticed at the distance of 5 or *600* yards, at least *3 times* our number of Savage looking fellows armed some with bows and arrows, some with lances and others with guns all mounted upon fiery steeds & charging to and fro just ready to make the attack: directly one advanced a few yards carrying a white flag & no Sooner was it perceived than answered by the elevation of a Sheepskin, which happened at the time to be the most convenient article. A talk ensued, the affair was amicably settled and soon about 3 dozen came into camp headed by the principal Chief of the whole tribe *"Mangus Colorado"* commonly known by the name of *"Red Sleeve."*[4] Tobacco was handed to the Indians which they were eager to get. They became quite friendly and conversed with us some knowing the spanish language to a certain degree. What seemingly interested them the utmost,

mines, to which Pownall apparently referred, were opened by Robert McKnight, one of the earliest Americans to engage in the Santa Fe trade, and later operated by his son-in-law, Lewis Flotte. Lack of fuel, water, and machinery and the constant danger of Indian raids seriously handicapped the operations of the properties.

[3] The town was situated near the eastern entrance to the important Guadalupe Pass that led through the Sierra Madre Mountains between Chihuahua and Sonora. Janos had been a garrison town of the Spaniards, but by Pownall's time it was rapidly going to pieces because of the Indians. See Glenn S. Dumke, ed., *Mexican Gold Trail* (San Marino, 1945), 138; John R. Bartlett, *Personal Narrative* . . . (2 vols., New York, 1854), II, 338–340; A. B. Clarke, *Travels in Mexico and California* (Boston, 1852), 61–72.

[4] This was Mangas Coloradas [Red Sleeves], the head chief of the Apaches. At the time Pownall wrote, Mangas, though the scourge of God to the Mexicans, usually befriended the Americans. Some years earlier, at the cost of a broken arm, he had saved the life of Benjamin D. Wilson, grandfather of General George S. Patton, from members of his own tribe. Mangas was killed in 1863 by soldiers of the California Column, under command of General J. R. West. There are several versions of the shooting, none of which reflects much credit on the Americans.

was our negro comrade as undoubtedly he was the first black man they had seen, several scrutinized his skin very closely. Leaving Yanos, we took a westerly course over a range of mountains which was rough and the country barren. Passed through Pelotaba. The next day we saw more Indians in the distance having an effect of spuring us on to St. Francis, where we camped over night and secured a few provisions. Our negro insisted that we get a large white flag and that he would carry it, which we did, that being a light cream cashmere shawl. From St. Francis we were three days ploughing through loose sandy soil making clouds of dust almost blinding us. Met a few Indians and arrived at San Bernardino June 28th.[5] It surely has been a tiresome journey since leaving Yanos a week ago. Our stock looks poor from lack of food and water. Some of the more ambitious men went hunting and exploring this evening, while the rest of us took to our blankets. Within a short time the men returned, rolling into camp a full barrel of mexican beverage, I believe called Mescal, it is probably made from cactus, grapes etc.[6] Most of us sampled it and was pleasant to take. Some drank it as though it was water. The effect worked like lightning throughout the camp. The barrel was soon emptied and it was way beyond midnight before rest was resumed. Oweing to this monotony breaker, we did not proceed on the trail until the early part of the after noon, headed for Black Water Creek 36 miles from here which was made in good time.[7] It was becoming dark on the evening of June 30th when we pitched camp. Yes indeed, Black water Creek has a very appropriate name. The only striking incident enroute was seeing numerous wild cattle. Had no difficulty in moving to the willows July 1st the weather being less suffocating. We are anxious to get out of mexico as it is understood that the climate and living accomodations are far better along the Pacific Coast and the Indians not so hostile. San Pedro was reached by 4-1/2 oclock in the afternoon on July 2nd. A picturesque little village situated along the San Pedro river.[8] The course of our next destination followed this same river endeavoring [enabling?] us to secure water easily. Independence day of America was celebrated struggling on through a long hot dusty and sandy trip from Santa Cruz to Santa Bar-

---

[5] An almost abandoned rancho. The company was now in the state of Sonora, just south of the present Arizona boundary. See "[Philip St. George] Cooke's Journal of the March of the Mormon Battalion, 1846–1847" in Ralph P. Bieber, ed., *Exploring Southwestern Trails* (Glendale, 1938), 132–133.

[6] A potent, widely used drink, distilled from the juice of the maguey plant.

[7] Presumably one of the headwaters of the Rio Sonora known as Agua Prieta.

[8] An important branch of the Gila River. See Cooke's Journal in Bieber, *Southwestern Trails,* 140–144. The river was well stocked with trout and the plain full of pugnacious wild bulls.

bara, covering 21 miles.[9] A most tiresome 100 miles over deserts and
mountains with but few villages other than La Vaca, Sopore, Long Post
and Tuscan [Tucson]. The later has now been reached July 11th. Another
100 miles or more of hot and hard procedure similar to that of a week
ago, with the last three days being trailless oweing to recent sand drifts.
Travelled northwest by compass. We occasionally met scantily clad Indians in small numbers. The Gila River is now before us July 17th. A
mighty good feeling to have plenty of water, there also being an abundance of salt grass and willows for the stock. It was midday of July 18th
before we could continue as several of the mules and horses were fastened
in a miry part of the river edge. Following the Gila River to where it
joins the Colorado river, was an easy task. We camped and prepared to
cross into the desired land of fortune, California. A raft was hurriedly
made to cross as the river was swift and deep. On the afternoon of July
19th many of the men and stock reached the opposite side. Early July 20th
the balance of the company crossed the river. We operated the raft with
a line of ropes. Two of our comrades, the last to come over could not
swim, were aboard the raft being pulled over. The rope snapped when
raft was in mid stream. Quick as a flash I. Messec of our company B swam
out and managed to get the rope fastened between his jaws, after a tiresome struggle landed them some distance down the river to safety.[10] July
21st 1849 with others my desire to stay and rest up a day or so along the
Colorado river was in vain as the majority were impatient and anxious
to get to the diggings. With as much extra water as we could carry oweing
to a dry stretch of approximately 100 miles to Carisso Creek, we covered
over no better country than the final 200 miles in Mexico.[11] It was in-
tensely hot during the days, the nights were disagreeably warm. Followed
the west edge of a desert area. Carisso Creek had very little to offer us on
account of the dry season. The water standing in pools I believed not
fit to drink so ordered it boiled before the men should drink it.[12] From
here on a comparatively miserable trip prevailed to Warners Ranch 51
miles distance.[13] Our entire company and stock are extremely exhausted.

[9] Originally a prosperous Spanish presidio, Santa Cruz in 1849 was "old, dilapidated and
the poorest of the poor"; but the valley itself was fertile, well-watered and timbered. Santa
Barbara was a long-abandoned rancho.

[10] I. G. Messec had been elected captain when Pownall's company left Keachie.

[11] A station of the Butterfield Overland Stage line was later established on this creek which
lies in eastern San Diego County.

[12] One of the few places in the diary where Pownall gives a hint of his medical training.

[13] Named for Jonathan Trumbull (Juan José) Warner, fur trader, ranchero, newspaper
editor, distinguished contributor to the making of Los Angeles. Warner's Ranch was one of
the best known and most welcome landmarks on the southern trail.

Had very little grub left when we paraded into this ranch. If not resembling a band of hungry wolves we surely felt likewise. Considerable buying trading and eating took place here. The day speeded away, leaving us with but sufficient time to only move 5 miles north. If I could think more clearly at present I would write more about the favuorable time extended to us at Warners Ranch but am too weary. The danger of losing our way is past, as a good wagon road to Pueblo Los Angeles and northern points of our route, we are assured of. Covering at an average of 20 miles a day through better country each day and more ranches that had a variety of fruit vegetables and meat, besides milk which many have missed in their coffee for the last moon or so. This afternoon August 3rd 1849 finds our company camping near the Pueblo Los Angeles. Much to my regret the order is to leave tomorrow noon August 4th. Last evening I enjoyed roaming about the town. Most of the business houses face a plaza where a seemingly carefree collection of mixed races assembled. Americans Mexicans Indians and others, Mexicans predominating. The Indians were mostly elaborately dressed, in fact some of the squaws had the appearance that of a rainbow if not a Christmas tree. It appeared like a festival was being held but learned it is just their merry mode of living. The town is of probably 2000 inhabitance.[14] No doubt a very thrifty center. Before departing I treated myself to a mighty fine meal, no, not in camp but in a 1st class eating house, also purchased a quart of brandy on the trip. With others I scrambled to get ready for the order to go. Left early in the afternoon, shy 2 of our comrades who may have taken a job or a drink too many. The area we have covered from Pueblo Los Angeles was considerably better comparative to the Rio Grande territory. On August 7th we were glorified by the sight of the Pacific Ocean. Its invigorating breeze swept up as if to greet us on the mountain top we had reached. Wild flowers, clover grass and trees were in abundance and plenty of good water as we descended to San Buena Ventura. A quaint village situated close to the Sea. The dwelling places were similiar to those in Mexico but had an added attraction of beautiful flower gardens enclosed by adobe walls. From here, we followed the sea shore to Santa Barbara arriving August 12th. In my opinion this town is a utopia.[15] It is beautifully nestled between hills protected from the sea. There is a large old mission with its gardens of fruit and flowers. With interest I observed the well trained and educated Indians of the mission. Some were engaged in painting religious subjects. We realize the grandeur of

---

[14] The Federal Census of 1850 gave the population as 1610.
[15] How right he was!

the country more each day, also that it costs more to live [the] further north we go. Much talk and excitement exists over many good reports about the gold diggings, causing us to hasten on. After leaving Santa Barbara, we drove by the seashore for approximately 35 miles, then taking a delightful pass through the hills into a valley which we followed to the sea. The weather being most pleasant during the day and the nights cool. Left sight of the ocean August 18th going inland to San Luis Obispo. Oweing to a curious incident that happened while at camp near San Luis Obispo, we have all been in a jolly spirit, due to the loss of company A's Captain's only pair of red flannel drawers which were taken from the wash line by a local goat or Indian. He needed them due to the cold foggy weather. After a drawerless day he complained of discomfort. Our good negro comrade suggested useing the cashmere shawl we had acquired for an Indian peace flag, to make the captain another pair. The task fell upon me. The Captain was very much delighted with the outcome, creating much merriment amongst us. This affair being the most fun we had enroute. Departing from San Luis Obispo, we climbed up a steep mountain over into a fertile valley which afforded us plenty of water and food for our stock. In a week we reached San Juan 150 miles north of San Luis Obispo.[16] August 27th pressed on from San Juan for Pueblo San Jose, another fertile valley endeavoring [enabling?] us to gain time, pitching camp at Pueblo San Jose August 29th. A meeting was held regarding a general split up, which was favorably decided upon and from here several different places were headed for, such as San Francisco, Sacramento Stockton etc. I remained here until Sept 1st when with 10 others left, going by the way of mission San Jose, thence through a canyon and over some small mountains, Had a severe struggle crossing the San Joaquin valley and up the foot hills due to the heat and being heavily laden with supplies. The ultimatum of our journey at last has been attained, arriving at Mariposa Diggings Friday September 7th 1849.[17] Pitched our camp on this far famed gold diggings of California and right glad too am I of it. We bid adieu for a season to pack mules, pack saddles etc. but in exchange therefore I fear we take upon our selves a still more onerous burden, that of crowbar, spade and pick.

---

[16] San Juan Bautista. The mission of this name, fifteenth among California missions, was founded June 24, 1797.

[17] One of the largest and most important of the so-called "Southern Mines." In 1844 Juan B. Alvarado received a grant of nearly 45,000 acres in this district and a few years later Frémont acquired most of the concession. The title and boundaries were the subject of long and costly litigation.

In a letter written February 22, 1850, Pownall adds this sequel to his arrival at the mines:

I arrived in the Mariposa diggings on the 7th Sept last, rather the worse for wear, nature worn perfectly thread bare & all the appliances of art unable to fulfil their vocation but hung together as if by magic. On the 2nd night my mules were stolen & I then had the pleasant reflection of finding myself homeless, friendless, penniless & confoundedly ragged and besides considerably in debt, for the means with which I supplied myself on starting were a little too scanty to carry me through.

To the very natural question of yours how have I succeeded since I came here I must candidly say, not quite as well as I expected for you are aware I believe that my calculations were somewhat up in the big figures. That there is gold here in abundance & scattered all over the Country no one who has ever been here will deny. To get it must needs require not only very hard work but a fair proportion of good luck also, the latter I consider quite essential: for one man may sink a hole in a portion of the diggings & without much trouble take out 1, 2, 3, 4 more ounces of dust daily, while his nearest neighbor off only a few feet, equally well accounted with all the necessary implements & withal quite as well raised, educated & good looking must content himself as well as he can with little or next to nothing. Nevertheless every manly untiring energy can manage to accumulate in the course of 12 mos what would be considered in any portion of the U. S. a very fair sum of money.

Across Mexico in '49

GLENN S. DUMKE

[Glenn S. Dumke is associate professor of history in Occidental College. His publications include *The Boom of the Eighties in Southern California* (San Marino, 1944) and *Mexican Gold Trail* (San Marino, 1945).]

OF ALL THOSE ARGONAUTS who traveled via overland trails to the California gold diggings in 1849, least attention has been paid to the ones who chose southern routes through the deserts of New Mexico or the hot lands and plateaus of Mexico itself. Despite this lack of attention, they comprised a considerable contingent. Ralph P. Bieber[1] estimates that some nine thousand took southern trails, and although no accurate figures are available, it seems reasonable to assume that more than half of these crossed the international border at some point in their journey. It is unfortunate that historians have not devoted more time to study of their odyssey, for their adventures were as colorful and vivid as were those of the Argonauts who plodded west by way of the Platte and the Humboldt.

Travelers who went through Mexico enjoyed several relative advantages. First, the mountains, which proved the bane of so many trans-Sierra expeditions, were generally lower and easier to negotiate in Mexico, and except for a few short, rugged passages, such as Guadalupe Pass, offered little hindrance. Weather, although hot and uncomfortable in desert regions, was seldom inclement enough to provide real danger on the order of Sierra snows or Death Valley aridity. Further, the routes through Mexico passed through better-settled regions than did many of the more northerly overland trails; this made food and fodder easier to obtain and provided shelter in case of illness. The Argonaut who selected the Mexican route usually was more comfortable and in less danger of his life.

Difficulties, however, were not lacking. The starting point for the Mexican journey was ordinarily the lower Mississippi Valley, often the city of New Orleans itself; and in 1849 cholera raged fiercely in that region and along the shores of the gulf, so that many hopeful adventurers found a quick end to their journey. Guides in Mexico were often unreliable and sometimes suggested little-known cutoffs which led only to trouble. In certain areas Apaches and Comanches threatened the travel-

---

[1] Ralph P. Bieber, ed., *Southern Trails to California in 1849* (Glendale, 1937), 62.

ers, although the Indians ordinarily limited their depredations to the Mexicans themselves. Mexican nationals, resentful of the outcome of the recently concluded war, sometimes grew belligerent and threatening, but most Americans in Mexico found that the general attitude was favorable. Finally, if the Argonaut chose the Durango-Mazatlán trail or one of the other routes that required water passage to San Francisco on the Pacific side, there was often some difficulty in finding accommodations on available vessels. Hindrances were plentiful but not overly menacing.

There were three main trails through Mexico, and innumerable variations of the three. The northernmost route crossed the Rio Grande in its lower reaches, at Brownsville, Roma, Laredo, or Eagle Pass, and plunged southwest. From any of the first three starting points, the usual trail was by way of Monterrey, Saltillo, and Parras, while travelers who crossed at Eagle Pass and Presidio del Rio Grande omitted Monterrey and Saltillo and joined the trail at Parras. From here the route led northwestward through the Bolsón de Mapimi to Chihuahua, thence to the wagon road blazed by Lieutenant Colonel Philip St. George Cooke during the Mexican War. This road led by way of Janos through Guadalupe Pass and Tucson to the Pima Villages on the Gila, and there the traveler joined the trail marked out by Colonel Stephen Kearny, which went westward via Yuma and the Colorado Desert to Warner's Ranch and San Diego. Variations of this route were taken mostly by travelers who left the Rio Grande farther north and joined the trail at Chihuahua or Corralitos, thus traversing Mexican territory for only a short distance,[2] others who turned west at Parral and went through Sonora instead of Chihuahua, and a few who took uncharted short cuts in various places.

The second main route followed the first as far as Parras, then, a short distance beyond, cut southwest through Durango to Mazatlán, where vessels were taken for San Francisco. The third trail traversed central Mexico, some of its travelers passing through Tampico and Guadalajara, thence to San Blas or Mazatlán on the west coast. Variations of this route included crossings of the continent at numerous southerly points.

These three routes, with their variants, were the chief trails by which forty-niners passed through Mexican territory on their way to the diggings. There is little evidence as to comparative popularity, but what there is seems to indicate that the northern route, via Monterrey and Saltillo, was the favorite. For months during the rush armed bands of emigrants, organized in semimilitary fashion, plodded with their pack

---

[2] For the northern and Durango-Mazatlán routes see end map in *ibid.*

trains and Mexican guides through the somnolent, dusty, whitewashed villages of Nuevo León and Chihuahua. The travelers attended religious pageants and were shocked, in pious, midwestern, Protestant manner, at the Roman Catholicism of the natives; they went eagerly to bullfights, and were equally horrified at what they saw. But still they came, denuding the little villages of food and fodder, marching by the dozens and hundreds toward the West.

In order to view this Mexican migration more thoroughly, four typical Argonauts will be considered: two who traveled by the northern trails, one by the Durango-Mazatlán cutoff, and the last by the central Mexico route.

John Durivage[3] was a correspondent of the New Orleans *Daily Picayune* who traveled with a party from the mouth of the Rio Grande via Monterrey, Saltillo, and Parras, through Chihuahua, and thence to the Gila trail. At Roma he encountered a bad epidemic of cholera. "Out of a whole population which cannot have exceeded forty souls, there have been about ten or twelve deaths," he reported to his editor.[4] "We have seen scarcely anything but suffering and death."[5] He was aware of the advantages of small parties for the Mexican journey:

... let me give a word of advice to all parties coming by this route. Do not form parties to exceed fifteen in number, as it will be difficult to procure subsistence and forage en route for larger ones. And above all, do not encumber yourselves with unnecessary baggage. No man's baggage, of all descriptions, ought to exceed one hundred and fifty pounds, and it is folly to bring any amount of provisions.[6]

A neighboring party encountered difficulty when its funds, some $12,000, vanished, and Durivage pointed out one questionable advantage of the cholera epidemic, when a man, seized with the dread disease, confessed that he had taken one-third of the sum. "He was rewarded for making a clean breast of it by recovering from the cholera, and I believe has not committed any other robbery as yet. This may in part be accounted for from the circumstance of his having been chained to a log ever since."[7]

Journeying on, Durivage encountered hot weather, numerous religious ceremonials, and shabby Mexican army garrisons. Monterrey, he

[3] See "Through Mexico to California," *ibid.*, 159–255. Another traveler who took the northern route and left an excellent account of his journey was A. B. Clarke, *Travels in Mexico and California* (Boston, 1852). See also the Pownall journal, in this issue.
[4] Bieber, *op. cit.*, 165.   [6] *Ibid.*, 167.
[5] *Ibid.*   [7] *Ibid.*, 169.

commented, had troops commanded by a general who boasted almost as many officers under him as men.[8] From Mier, near the Rio Grande, the Argonauts went to Chicherone, where water was obtainable despite drought conditions that prevailed throughout most of the region, thence to Punta Aguda, a village wrecked by soldiery and bandits. Food, in the form of corn, barley, eggs, dried beef, and "miserable coffee"[9] was available at "two bits a meal"; and Durivage noted that the Mexicans were generous and well-disposed toward Americans, who "have behaved themselves and respected the Mexicans, and have consequently left a most favorable impression wherever they have passed."[10]

Between Cerralvo and Marín was a *jornada,* or dry march, and Monterrey lay twenty-five miles beyond. Monterrey was a fairly large town, but its suburbs were not kept up, and Durivage viewed with interest a throng gathered before a butcher shop, clinking coins on tin plates, watching the *carnero,* bloody and disheveled, cutting up a beef. He traveled to Saltillo by way of Rinconada, noted for its thieving inhabitants. Saltillo had paved streets, two-story houses painted in warm colors, and a population of fifteen thousand. He then passed the battlefield of Buena Vista, where General Taylor had won a signal victory in the Mexican War, and, by way of Angostura Pass and a mountainous trail, went to Parras, a prosperous city with substantial buildings and an attractive plaza.

From Parras, two roads pointed to Chihuahua: one poor and without water, via El Pozo; and another, usable by wagons, by way of La Peña and El Álamo. Several large ranches intervened on the way to Mapimi, and the trail passed close by silver smelters. Durivage passed through Las Cruces and Cerro Gordo, and finally arrived in Chihuahua on April 30, by way of Santa Cruz de Rosales, scene of another Mexican War battle. From Chihuahua the way was clearly marked to Cooke's road and the Gila. This route, because of its numerous towns and abundance of provisions, was favored by many emigrants.

Some travelers taking this northern route were delayed by the advice of unreliable guides. One such was George Evans, an attorney of Defiance, Ohio, who was misled into a little-known desert trail north of Saltillo and Parras and was forced to cross the wastelands of the Serranía del Burro.[11] Like many others, Evans and his companions journeyed down

[8] *Ibid.,* 171.
[9] *Ibid.,* 171–172.
[10] *Ibid.*
[11] George W. B. Evans, *Mexican Gold Trail: The Journal of a Forty-Niner,* Glenn S. Dumke, ed. (San Marino, 1945).

the Mississippi to New Orleans, and took ship for Matagorda Bay in Texas. He landed at Port Lavaca, then an important terminus for Argonauts, and went overland through Texas by way of Victoria, Goliad, and San Antonio to Eagle Pass and Presidio del Rio Grande. On April 21 he crossed the international boundary and entered Mexico. He and his companions reorganized themselves into one of the semimilitary bands so characteristic of gold seekers' expeditions, and, calling themselves the Ohio Company, joined another and larger group, the Mississippi Mining Company, for the Mexican passage.

Cholera had plagued the travelers since their arrival in New Orleans, and another member of the party fell victim just as the Ohio Company entered Mexico; Evans contributed a gem to gold-rush records by listing in detail the equipment of the unfortunate victim.[12] The party traversed fertile lands near the border made memorable by General Wool's Mexican War expedition, and crossed the Sabinas River to Santa Rosa. Here, instead of continuing southward to Saltillo and Parras as did the majority, Evans and his party took the advice of a guide who recommended striking out northwestward directly across the barren uplands of the Serranía del Burro by way of a little-known pass called Santana. The country grew drier and more difficult as they progressed, the few water holes being shallow and alive with organisms. At one pool the travelers had to strain baby mosquitoes through their teeth, and another was composed of "one third green, fine moss, one third polliwogs, and one third embryo mosquitoes—and but a little of that."[13] Relics of depredations by Indians were numerous on the trail, consisting largely of the bones of stolen and slaughtered cattle. On May 24 the sufferings of the group reached their climax. The party split and scattered, searching for water:

We pushed onward, however, Mr. Parker falling in the rear—and in a few miles more he was lost to sight, his mules failing very fast. Our poor animals became more and more exhausted every hour, and I was reflecting on the propriety of abandoning my pack when we were met by Dr. Riley returning to the last water, then a distance of about forty miles. He told us that Watson's wagons were about two miles ahead, the mules all turned loose and the men scattered in every direction, and some dying of thirst. By this time I had become very much exhausted, my mouth and tongue parched and much swollen. We reached the wagons after another hour's severe toiling, and found men in absolute despair, having abandoned the idea of immediate or prospective relief. As soon as our animals were relieved of their loads, we took such shelter as the wagons afforded from the rays of a burning sun, and here in fitful and

[12] *Ibid.*, 48 n.
[13] *Ibid.*, 60.

agonising slumber passed about two hours. Our minds wandered back to the cool and refreshing streams and springs at our loved homes—. . . but to be called back to the miserable reality of our forlorn and apparently hopeless condition, by some one crying in the agony of his soul, "Water, oh, God, some water!"[14]

This eighty-mile *jornada* finally came to an end, however, and with the loss of only one member of the party, who wandered off crazed by thirst, the Ohio Company approached the valley of the Rio Conchos and arrived at Presidio San Carlos on June 7. Although they were suspicious of their guide's loyalty, and were convinced that he was planning to betray them to the Indians for plunder, he proved to be more honest than competent.

Originally they had intended to go directly westward to Chihuahua from San Carlos, but an error in reckoning led them northward to Presidio del Norte, and they were then forced to double back down the Conchos Valley. The land grew more attractive, and finally Evans and his companions camped in the outskirts of Chihuahua, the metropolis of northwestern Mexico. Chihuahua boasted a picturesque location on a plain surrounded by rocky mountains, a great cathedral of cut stone, a mint, and a large bullfight arena. It had "wide clean streets, and handsome buildings. . . . The plaza or public square, is large and imposing, adorned with a splendid fountain and seats, and pillars of white porphyry."[15] Many American merchants maintained contacts in Chihuahua, and business was brisk.

On July 18 Evans and his group left Chihuahua and moved northward across the vast estate owned by politician Don Angel Trias, to Galeana and the majestic ruins of Casa Grande. The trail blazed by Lieutenant Colonel Cooke then led northward to Janos and westward through rugged Guadalupe Pass, near the present international border. The pass presented some difficulties to wagon travel. "The hills," said Evans, "are steep and rugged and the deep, dark and gloomy ravines almost numberless, and the mountain sides covered with a growth of low and heavy-topped trees."[16] The road then took them to San Bernardino Rancho, where wild cattle were "dangerous as the buffalo,"[17] and thence via Tucson to the Pima-Maricopa villages on the Gila. These Indians, with their sedentary, industrious agriculture, impressed Evans much more than did the raiding-camp Indians farther south. From the Gila

---

[14] *Ibid.*, 64–65.   [16] Evans, *op. cit.*, 143.
[15] Clarke, *op. cit.*, 51.   [17] *Ibid.*, 145.

westward the trail followed Emory's route, and difficulties were less severe, despite the Colorado Desert crossing. Evans merits attention because of his excellent and detailed descriptions of the Mexican route and because he allowed himself to be persuaded into taking one of the little-known cutoffs which rendered this ordinarily safe northern trail sometimes distinctly hazardous.

The third traveler to be considered is Samuel McNeil, a cobbler who chose the Saltillo-Durango-Mazatlán route, ending with a sea passage to San Francisco.[18] McNeil started from Lancaster, Ohio, with a party of twelve men, on February 7, 1849. He journeyed down the Mississippi and intended, at New Orleans, to travel to California via the Isthmus of Panama, but the vessel, heading for Chagres, developed a leak and instead landed its passengers at Brazos, at the mouth of the Rio Grande. McNeil's group hired a guide and interpreter here for $300, to lead them to Mazatlán; and the journey through Monterrey, Saltillo, and Parras duplicated many of Durivage's experiences. West of Parras, however, McNeil left the northern trail, and struck southwestward to Quinquema. On the road the party saw nine Comanches attack a mule train laden with silver, convoyed by thirty Mexicans, on its way to Durango. The Indians left the silver on the ground and drove off the mules—their chief objective—and the Mexicans fled to the protection of the Americans after one of their number had been slain. The alcalde of Quinquema offered fifty dollars to each member of McNeil's party if they would pursue the Comanches, but the group, hesitating to get into the bad graces of the Indians, considering the long journey ahead, decided against it. After they departed from Quinquema, the Mexicans sallied out and did battle with the Comanches, the casualties being five Mexicans killed and twelve wounded, and one Indian killed.[19]

On April 19, McNeil and his party arrived in Durango, a city with about 125,000 population. "The houses," he said, "look like prisons, the doors and windows being plentifully supplied with iron bars, as if to prevent the beaux from carrying off the ladies or the Indians from capturing the whole family."[20] The town also had splendid churches—"On entering one of them I thought that I had prematurely got into California, so valuable and splendid were the ornaments glittering with real gold and silver."[21] Like most other Argonauts in Mexico, McNeil went to a bullfight, along with some three thousand others, and saw, with proper

---

[18] Samuel McNeil, *McNeil's Travels in 1849 to, through, and from the Gold Regions in California* (Columbus, 1850)

[19] *Ibid.*, 15–16.   [20] *Ibid.*, 16.   [21] *Ibid.*

disgust, six bulls and three horses killed and one Mexican wounded. At Durango the party sold its wagons and mules, and exchanged them for a mule pack train for the 160-mile journey to Mazatlán.[22]

West of Durango, mountains were encountered, and one of the Argonauts timidly dismounted from his mule and drove it before him on the narrow trail. McNeil defiantly stayed in the saddle, remarking that he did not intend to pay a dollar a day for the privilege of driving a mule over the mountains. They came into volcanic country, with lava outcrops, hot springs, and other evidence of subterranean activity. On the fifth day out of Durango the party got a glimpse of the Pacific Ocean from a summit. Active silver mines were passed, food in the villages was plentiful and good, and the journey was not at all unpleasant.

At Mazatlán, which, McNeil estimated, had a population of about ten thousand, the group found a French brig and a Danish schooner. McNeil took passage on the schooner, paying seventy-five dollars for passage to San Francisco. The small vessel took on two hundred passengers and served them such bad food—"wormy bread, putrid jerked beef, musty rice, and miserable tea"[23]—that the passengers mutinied and threatened violence to the captain, who, enraged in turn, promised to return them all to Mazatlán. The passengers, however, warned him that they would shoot him if he changed the vessel's course, and the officer, subdued, improved the rations somewhat. The uncomfortable passage required twenty days, and McNeil's greeting in San Francisco was a breakfast which cost, to his shocked amazement, two dollars and a half. McNeil's route was probably the easiest of all the Mexican trails, as it avoided the worst deserts of the northern route and clung to fairly well-settled country. The sole difficulty was the sea passage on the Pacific side.

The fourth Argonaut to have a place in this sketch is Daniel Woods, a Philadelphian who journeyed by sea to Tampico on the Gulf coast and made his way overland to the Pacific port of San Blas, where he took ship for San Francisco.[24] His route illustrates the central Mexico road, and was probably second only to McNeil's in ease of accomplishment, the one added difficulty being a satisfactory sea passage on the Atlantic side.

Woods and his party of forty started February 1, 1849, at the foot of Arch Street in Philadelphia and boarded the bark *Thomas Walters* for Tampico. They arrived there without incident on February 21, where they were "most happy to exchange the monotony, the junk and other

---

[22] *Ibid.*, 17.
[23] *Ibid.*, 20.
[24] Daniel B. Woods, *Sixteen Months at the Gold Diggings* (London, 1851).

salt provisions, and the green waves of a sea life, for the pleasing variety, the delicious fruits and vegetables, and the beautiful fields of a tropical climate."[25] The group passed its first night on Mexican soil in a vacant theater building and then, while making arrangements for the land journey, spent a few days in spearing fish and shooting deer and alligators. Insects were so bad, Woods said, that he had to live with his gloves on and adopted the practice of sleeping in a light cotton bag which he tied over his head. Tampico was a city of about seven thousand people, with many Americans in business; a former Ohio farmer, for instance, supplied Woods and his party with mules for the trip to the west coast.

The mule train set out across the level plains of the Tierra Caliente, then, after a few days, began to ascend the eastern slopes of the Sierra Madre. They encountered heavy forests and towns wrecked by revolution and banditry. Woods was apparently a Roman Catholic, unlike many travelers through Mexico, and he bore with him a letter in Latin from the Bishop of Philadelphia, which was endorsed in Spanish by the *padre* of Villa del Valle. Woods's commentary is generally more respectful toward Mexican religious customs than were those of his Protestant contemporaries.

Mexican ways of life still amused and shocked the foreigners, however. The practice of mixed bathing in the rivers was a matter for detailed comment, and the prevalence of brigands and the even greater prevalence of reports of lurking highwaymen caused comment and speculation of another sort. The mountains were volcanic in nature with pumice rock which was hard on the mules' shoes, and the party added to its difficulties by taking one report of highway robbery seriously and departing from the main road for a little-used detour in the highlands. Even here, however, occasional crosses by the side of the trail testified to the activity of outlaws, and at one rocky abutment the party was surprised by six men who were lying in wait for chance travelers. The size of the Argonaut group, however, together with its calm resoluteness and numerous arms, frightened off the bandits.

They finally reached the plateau of central Mexico, eight thousand feet above sea level. Here they passed through a stretch of desert which welcomed them with a terrible dust storm. Woods's description of this event is worth repeating:

It was near night. We saw before us, which after a time spread out all around us, many wild whirlwinds which extended up into the sky, carrying with them

[25] *Ibid.*, 21.

apparently solid conical masses of clouds. We counted upward of sixty cones formed and forming at the same time. As the sun was setting, these extended at the top, opening something in the form of an umbrella, the cones still continuing to play up their heaving masses into its expanding bosom, which presented a most unearthly and terrific appearance. It was the *blackness of darkness,* which suddenly became illuminated by the lurid flashes of lightning darting through it, and forming a picture of that wrath which, we may suppose, broods and bursts over the bottomless pit.[26]

The dust was so thick at the height of the storm that breathing was difficult, and it thoroughly permeated clothing and packs. The party gained shelter in a near-by *mesón,* typical of the inns in Mexico in that it was built about a court and featured twenty-foot-square unfurnished rooms for the convenience of travelers, who were expected to provide their own bedding and supplies. Meals could be obtained at a near-by *fonda.* Guests brought their own utensils, and were served peppery soups, rice, tortillas, fried squash, rice or chocolate custard, and coffee, wine, or pulque, according to their tastes. Both inn and restaurant were vermin infested, and tarantulas hung on the sleeping-room walls.

The groups halted in San Luís Potosí, a silver-mining center which was connected with Mexico City by stage. Woods talked to a local schoolmaster, who believed his stories about steamships but refused to credit the Yanqui's tale of the telegraph. At another time, Woods and some companions were walking down a city street when they saw an attractive *señorita* seated by a grilled window. They greeted her courteously, and she nodded and smiled in return, then—to their surprise—emitted a terrible oath and some obscene phrases completely at variance with her amiable expression. The Americans discovered later that a Yankee soldier, as a practical joke, had taught her these words as terms of greeting—a prank often repeated in Mexico.

On April 2 the party reached Guadalajara, the largest city on their route. The town had beautiful and large buildings, huge churches, iron-grated windows, fortress-like doors, and countless bell towers. "In this city," said Woods, "we were first made rather painfully aware of a custom of the country, of uncovering the head while passing the front portal of the cathedral. Two or three stones, well aimed, removed the hats which our hands should have removed."[27] Through the mountainous country west of Guadalajara, Woods and his companions passed, in time for much of the Easter ceremonial in several of the towns. They

[26] *Ibid.,* 28.
[27] *Ibid.,* 34.

came upon a charred field in which was a gallows bearing three victims and a sign, *"Así castiga la ley al ladrón y al asesino."* There were more bandit scares, additional mountain climbing, then a final descent from the plateau to San Blas on the Pacific shore. Here the company dissolved: "Men alone," Woods bemoaned, "are not social beings, and the numerous attempts to bind them together in California gold-mining associations are as vain as the attempt to make a rope of sand."[28]

At San Blas the party took passage on the *San Blasiña,* a twenty-three-ton schooner. The disagreeableness of the voyage to Mazatlán recalled to Woods's mind the tales he had heard of eager Argonauts embarking from Panama in whaleboats for San Francisco. The comforts offered by the *San Blasiña* were not much better; three members of the party, including Woods himself, slept on deck in a lashed dugout, his bunk space measuring 2½ by 3½ feet. At Mazatlán the group encountered a crowd awaiting passage for San Francisco, and as the owners of the schooner had not fulfilled the terms of their contract, the Argonauts took over title to the vessel. Departing from Mazatlán on May 4 with an elderly, incompetent captain, the vessel set off to cross the gulf and round Cape San Lucas. The going was slow, however, owing to the captain's incompetence, and Woods claimed that the French mate had to correct the course surreptitiously every night after the commander had retired. Because of water shortage, a landing in whaleboats was attempted at San José, and some of the passengers were almost drowned in the shark-infested waters. Finally, so much trouble was encountered in rounding the cape that another anchorage was found and some of the party deserted, most to travel by land up the Pacific coast of the peninsula, Woods and three others choosing the Gulf shore. The Woods group eventually happened upon a Scottish bark at San José and booked passage for San Francisco. After thirty days aboard this vessel they landed at the Embarcadero on June 25, 1849.

These brief sketches but sample the literature of Mexican travel in 1849. Because Mexico was a settled country, innumerable variations of the trails were possible; these four Argonauts by no means exhausted the adventures and topography offered by the Mexican routes. Notwithstanding the relative ease and comfort of the Mexican journey, adventures were possible, and the normal perils of the trail were by no means absent.

The traveler who made the best time record was McNeil (February 7

[28] *Ibid.,* 39.

to May 30), who arrived in San Francisco a little more than three and a half months after he set out. The slowest, by all odds, was Evans, who took nearly eight months, from February 20 to October 18, to reach San José. These figures bear out other evidence in supporting the apparent fact that the Saltillo-Durango-Mazatlán route was probably the easiest, with the central Mexico route second in convenience, and the northern trails and their variations most difficult and longest.

With the exception of Bieber and a few others, analysts of the gold rush have dipped but shallowly into the abundant literature of these trails. And yet this part of the great odyssey possesses added interest because of its incursion into a foreign land. The Argonaut who traveled through Mexico may have enjoyed a slightly easier journey, but his difficulties and hardships were numerous and his accomplishments as great as any of those who took the trail to California in '49.

The Gold Rush by Panama, 1848-1851

JOHN HASKELL KEMBLE

[Associate professor of history in Pomona College and secretary-treasurer of the Pacific Coast Branch of the American Historical Association, John Haskell Kemble is the author of *The Panama Route, 1848–1869* (Berkeley, 1943).]

WITH THE FULL confirmation of the richness of the California placers in December, 1848, young men throughout the settled parts of the United States began making plans to set out for the fabulous foothills of the Sierra Nevada. At that time of year there were only two routes of travel open to California. One was by sea around Cape Horn to San Francisco Bay. The other was by water to some port on the coast of Mexico or Central America, overland to the Pacific, and then by water once more to California. Trails across the continent from the Missouri River to California, although they eventually would carry the greatest number of emigrants, were closed by snow when news of the gold discovery reached the United States, and it would not be feasible to start on them until late in the spring of 1849.

There were arguments both for and against both of these available routes. The Cape Horn route took more time, but it was less complicated in that the emigrant stayed in the same ship all the way. Although part of the course lay through notoriously rough seas, events proved that the traveler who chose this route was surest of reaching California alive and in good health. There were several isthmian crossings which were theoretically feasible: Panama, Nicaragua, Guatemala, Tehuantepec, and Central Mexico. Of these, however, only that at Panama received extensive use during the gold rush. Although it required longer sea voyages than the other isthmian crossings, it offered the shortest land journey, and at Panama the arrangements to facilitate the journey from sea to sea were more nearly complete. The principal drawbacks of this route lay in the climate and hardships of travel on the isthmus, and the insufficiency of ships on the Pacific to carry passengers from Panama to San Francisco.

Of the passengers arriving in 1849 at San Francisco, 15,597 had come round Cape Horn, as compared with 6,489 by way of Panama. The latter route gained quickly in popularity, however, as its advantages of speed became known and ignorance concerning it was dispelled. Thus in 1850 there were 11,770 arrivals by way of the Horn and 13,809 by

Panama.[1] In 1852 more than 20,000 traveled to San Francisco by way of Panama, and the number continued to be usually between 15,000 and 20,000 a year until the completion of the transcontinental railroad in 1869.[2] At the same time, the Cape Horn route declined in popularity as a passenger carrier, although it continued to be of great importance for the transportation of cargo to and from California.

The aim of this paper is to describe the Panama route, and particularly the isthmian crossing, as it was in the years 1849 and 1850, rather than to review its whole history. By 1851 the most acute problems of transportation on the Pacific and of organization of travel on the isthmus had been overcome. Although it was not until the completion of the Panama Railroad in 1855 that the journey between the oceans ceased to have a good deal of the air of adventure, the passing of the crest of the gold rush coincided with the firm establishment of the Panama route as a fully accepted means of travel between California and the rest of the United States.

The Isthmus of Panama first became a major highway between the oceans in the early sixteenth century. Gold and silver from the mines of Peru came by sea to Panama, and there they were loaded on muleback to be carried across to Porto Bello for shipment on to Spain. With the coming of independence in the early nineteenth century, traffic to and from the west coast of South America shifted to the Cape Horn route, and the trail across the Isthmus of Panama fell into disuse.

Revival began in 1845, when steamers of the Pacific Steam Navigation Company, which had been operating on the west coast of South America since 1840, extended their voyages north to Panama. Another British firm, the Royal Mail Steam Packet Company, had steamers which came from England to the Caribbean and were already making regular calls on the Atlantic coast of the isthmus. Together the companies provided a through service from England to the west coast of South America using the Panama link. The arrangements made to transport passengers and baggage across the isthmus for this service were those which the first California-bound travelers found when they arrived there at the end of 1848.

In 1848 two steamship lines were established under the auspices of the United States government which together offered through passage

---

[1] Records made by Edward S. King, harbor master at San Francisco, and published in Willard B. Farwell, "Cape Horn and Coöperative Mining in '49," *Century Magazine*, n.s., XX, 593.

[2] John Haskell Kemble, *The Panama Route, 1848–1869* (Berkeley and Los Angeles, 1943), 254.

from the Atlantic and Gulf coasts to California. These were the United States Mail Steamship Company and the Pacific Mail Steamship Company. The former dispatched its first steamer from New York for the isthmus in December, 1848, and the pioneer vessel of the latter was scheduled to sail from Panama for California and Oregon in January of the next year.[3] Although these companies were established well before knowledge of the 1848 gold discovery reached the United States, it so happened that their ships were ready to take up their service at the very moment of the outbreak of the mania to head for the riches which were apparently so easily obtainable in California.

For the prospective traveler to California by way of Panama, there was little detailed information available concerning the nature of the route which he would take or the preparations necessary for it. The most reliable data to be had at the beginning of the gold rush were contained in a guidebook by an Englishman, John Osborne, designed for the use of passengers on the steamers of the Royal Mail.[4] It was based on materials furnished by agents of the company, and it described the isthmian crossing with some accuracy and detail. Conditions at Panama changed rapidly with the beginning of the tide of emigration to California, and Osborne's book soon became out of date, its descriptions of quiet, leisurely travel in the tropics contrasting sharply with the state of affairs on the isthmus in 1849 and the years following.

In the last month of 1848, and during 1849, 1850, and 1851 at least two or three dozen California guidebooks appeared in the United States, and a few were also published in England, France, and Germany. Most of the early ones were compilations which leaned heavily on recently published official reports and other accounts available in print, and only a handful contained any really useful information relative to the Panama crossing. The best of the 1849 guides for this route was probably that written by George Alexander Thompson, and published in London under the auspices of the Royal Mail.[5] It drew on Osborne, but also contained new material which described conditions after the beginning of the California migration. The 1849 guides by Disturnell, Thurston, and

[3] *Ibid.*, 12–30.

[4] John Osborne, *Guide to the West Indies, Madeira, Mexico, Northern South-America, &c., &c. Compiled from Documents Specially Furnished by the Agents of the Royal Mail Steam Packet Company, the Board of Trade, and Other Authentic Sources* (4th ed., London, 1846). Hereafter cited as Osborne, *Guide.*

[5] George Alexander Thompson, *Hand Book to the Pacific and California, Describing Eight Different Routes, by Sea, Central America, Mexico, and the Territories of the United States, Particularly with Reference to the Ports Frequented by the Steamers of the Royal Mail Steam Packet Company* (London, 1849). Hereafter cited as Thompson, *Hand Book.*

Ware, although not based on personal experience, also contained useful information on the Panama route.[6]

Early in 1850 Joseph W. Gregory published a guidebook which surpassed earlier books in that Gregory, the proprietor of an express company operating between California and the Atlantic coast, had made the isthmian trip more than once himself, and was able to give good advice based on this experience.[7]

In the following year, 1851, Dr. E. L. Autenrieth published a guide devoted exclusively to the Panama crossing.[8] This book, apparently the most detailed of its kind, ran to fourteen pages of text, and although it left many matters untouched, it was the best thing of the sort to appear during the gold rush years.

In addition to these guidebooks, the accounts of travelers to and from California as published in books and newspapers in 1849 and the years following were very useful to the prospective emigrant. They were obviously written with a view to instructing and aiding those about to go over the route as well as to entertaining stay-at-homes.

Whatever instructions they had, and most of them were very ill-prepared for the journey, travelers bound for California began to arrive on the Isthmus of Panama at the end of 1848. On December 27 the steamer *Falcon* of the United States Mail Steamship Company reached Chagres with nearly 200 passengers from New York and New Orleans. On the twenty-ninth the bark *John Benson* came in from New York with 50 more. By the end of May, 1849, some 59 vessels had arrived at Chagres, bringing nearly 4,000 passengers.[9] Of the 59, 42 were under sail, and only 17 were steamers; but the greater size, speed, and regularity of the latter gave them a great advantage over sailing vessels in attracting passengers, and they were presently carrying almost the entire trade. By

[6] J. Disturnell, *The Emigrant's Guide to New Mexico, California, and Oregon; Giving the Different Overland and Sea Routes* . . . (New York, 1849); William Thurston, *Guide to the Gold Regions of Upper California* (London, 1849); Joseph Ware, *The Emigrants' Guide to California, Containing Every Point of Information for the Emigrant* . . . (St. Louis, 1849).

[7] Joseph W. Gregory, *Gregory's Guide for California Travellers; via the Isthmus of Panama. Containing All the Requisite Information Needed by Persons Taking this Route* . . . (New York, 1850). Hereafter cited as Gregory, *Guide*. Gregory devotes five pages to advice for travelers.

[8] E. L. Autenrieth, *A Topographical Map of the Isthmus of Panama, together with a Separate and Enlarged Map of the Lines of Travel, and also a Map of the City of Panama* . . . *with a Few Accompanying Remarks for the Use of Travellers* (New York, 1851). Hereafter cited as Autenrieth, *Guide*.

[9] New York *Herald*, March 4, May 12, 1849. The ports of origin of these vessels were as follows: New York, 31; New Orleans, 17; Boston, 4; Baltimore, 2; Philadelphia, 1; Charleston, 1; Norfolk, 1; St. Augustine, 1.

the early part of 1851 there were 13 steamers operating regularly from New York and New Orleans to Chagres, with a total capacity of almost 5,000 passengers.[10]

After a voyage of eight to twelve days if he came from New York, or of less than a week if New Orleans were his port of departure, the traveler sighted the jungle-covered coast of the Isthmus of Panama, frequently veiled in rain, as his ship approached her anchorage off the mouth of the Chagres River. Since the end of the colonial period, the Porto Bello road had been abandoned in favor of a route up the Chagres from the sea to a point about twenty miles from the city of Panama, whence trails struck overland for the remaining distance.

Since the depth over the bar at the mouth of the Chagres was only about 13 feet, ocean-going vessels had to lie off the coast while their passengers landed in small boats or were transferred in the ship's boats to the small steamer *Orus,* which sometimes acted as tender in 1849 and 1850. The price of landing passengers and their baggage was included in the ticket in 1850, but the next year every traveler was paying $2.00 to be carried ashore.[11]

In 1848 the town of Chagres consisted of a few thatched huts, inhabited only by Indians and Negroes, except for a handful of government officials. It stood on the right bank of the river in the shadow of Castle San Lorenzo, a magnificent fortification built in the eighteenth century to guard the mouth of the river. Osborne wrote that there was "a house, called an hotel, kept by Peter Eskildsen, who professed to use 'his utmost endeavours to facilitate to travellers all the conveniences that the country will permit of.' "[12]

With the beginning of the California migration, Chagres underwent a great change. An "American" settlement, also called Chagres, sprang up across the river from the older town, and this became the landing place as well as the point of departure for the journey up the river. Like a hundred other short-lived towns on routes of pioneer travel, Chagres burgeoned with frame hotels, saloons, and dwellings, displaying "young Yankee-dom abroad in full strength, not caring even for the worst climate in all America."[13] There were three or four hotels at Chagres by the end

[10] The following steamers operated from New York: *Cherokee, Crescent City, Eldorado, Empire City, Georgia, North America, Ohio,* and *Prometheus.* The steamers running regularly from New Orleans up to the early part of 1851 were: *Alabama, Falcon, Mexico, Pacific,* and *Philadelphia.*

[11] Gregory, *Guide,* 4; Panama *Star,* February 11, 1851.

[12] Osborne, *Guide,* 256.

[13] Autenrieth, *Guide,* 5–6.

of 1849, and a small, fairly permanent white population of steamship and express agents, bartenders, and hotelkeepers. It was an important enough place to warrant the establishment of a United States consulate in 1850.[14] A resident of the isthmus wrote of Chagres: "I do not know of any one you can get to come here who will not be sick part of the time. Most persons at Chagres become dissipated in a few weeks; and between drinking too much, running after women, or gambling, exhaust all their energies, and when they get sick, they have no vitality left in their systems to recover."[15] Guidebooks and travelers agreed that the climate of Chagres was execrable—hot, humid, and windless—and urged the Argonaut to get out of town as soon as possible. Osborne, writing in unhurried days before the gold rush, recommended the immediate hiring of a small canoe or *cayuco*, capable of carrying one passenger together with a couple of trunks and a cot. If the traveler had more luggage, he could easily hire another *cayuco* to carry it. The cost of the trip from Chagres to the head of navigation should not, Osborne wrote, exceed $10.[16] As travel increased, the desirability of leaving Chagres as soon as possible after landing from the steamer did not change, but boats on the river came to be in greater demand, and the prices charged by native boatmen rose. At the beginning of 1849, the rate for a single *cayuco* had increased to $50, and for a larger dugout canoe which would carry four or five passengers it was about $10 a person.[17] By the end of 1849 this type of craft cost $30 to $40 for a trip, and this rate remained fairly constant until early 1851.[18]

Dr. Autenrieth advised travelers to make written contracts with the boatmen, "which can always be easily accomplished by stipulating in the receipt for the money you advance to the boatmen, the time in which they have to bring you to the different places along the river."[19] Passengers found that the Indians and Negroes who paddled and poled the boats were prone to suggest frequent stops, and that once they were out of the boat it was hard to get them back into it again. Firm refusals of these requests, and insistence that the boatmen eat their lunches in the boat rather than go ashore for them helped to insure good progress.

---

[14] Index, Dispatches from Consuls Mexico, New Granada, Venezuela, Ecuador, December 28, 1828–December 19, 1853, No. 5, pp. 366–367, MS, National Archives. Hereafter cited as Index, Dispatches. The consulate was moved to Aspinwall in March, 1852.

[15] Henry Tracy to M. O. Roberts, Chagres, February 24, 1851, in Superior Court, New York, *William Heilman* versus *Marshall O. Roberts* (New York, 1861), 272. Hereafter cited as *Heilman* vs. *Roberts*.

[16] Osborne, *Guide*, 256–257.

[17] New York *Herald*, January 25, 31, 1849.

[18] Gregory, *Guide*, 4–5; Panama *Star*, February 11, 1851.

[19] Autenrieth, *Guide*, 7.

The guidebooks urged travelers to provide themselves with bedding and to remain in their boats at night. There were, however, accommodations ashore along the Chagres. At Gatun, eight miles above the sea, there were two huts, called hotels, kept by Americans. Farther along, at Los Dos Hermanos, "friendly and obliging Americans" offered lodgings, and at Palenquilla, twenty-eight miles above Chagres, there was another "Hotel, where you find a place to sleep, and bad food at high prices."[20] In an emergency, food and shelter could be had at native houses along the river, although these were generally "poor 'sights' for hungry travellers," and a person planning to remain over night was advised to provide his own hammock.[21]

Fowls, eggs, and sometimes milk, as well as coffee and some cooked food could be purchased from the natives, but the guide books advised travelers to bring food and drink with them from the steamer. Thompson not only suggested that the ship's larder be raided to the tune of roast duck, boiled tongue, sherry, pale ale, and brandy, but recommended that Argonauts bring along an "Etna" portable stove which burned spirits of alcohol and on which tea could be brewed and eggs boiled.[22]

The trip up the Chagres by canoe usually took three days to Gorgona, which was 39½ miles from the mouth of the river. Cruces, although only four and a half miles farther up, was an additional day's trip because of the increasingly swift current. During the dry season, from December to June, the trip up the river had much to recommend it, presenting "to northern people a great variety of interesting and novel sights; even the dullest intellect is compelled to remark the different vegetation, and the great variety of birds with most beautiful plumage." The heavy showers which fell almost constantly during the wet season rendered the trip uncomfortable, even in a covered boat, and the often swollen river was difficult and sometimes dangerous to negotiate.[23]

Almost as soon as the heavy stream of travel began to cross the isthmus, there were efforts to improve the primitive conditions obtaining there. The second steamer to reach Chagres from New York was the *Orus*, a 247-ton craft which had formerly done duty on the Shrewsbury River between New York and Red Bank and was now intended for service up the Chagres. Her draft, however, was too deep to permit her to ascend

---

[20] *Ibid.,* 7–8.
[21] Thompson, *Hand Book,* 17–19; Gregory, *Guide,* 4–5.
[22] Thompson, *Hand Book,* 17–19.
[23] Autenrieth, *Guide,* 8, 11.

more than twenty miles or so above its mouth. At that, she could shorten
the river trip by carrying travelers as far as she could and towing their
baggage in canoes astern. In the summer of 1849, the stern-wheeler *General
Herran* appeared on the river, and in 1850 the *Raphael Rivas, Henry
Gleason, Gorgona,* and *Swan* followed. The *Millie* and the *William H.
Aspinwall* joined the river fleet in 1851. Most of these were not very successful, although some were able to make the trip through to Gorgona
in wet season when the river was high.[24] A line of ship's boats, fitted in
"New York fashion" was also on the river in 1850. There were forty of
these in the fall of that year, and they reportedly nearly drove the native
dugouts out of business.[25]

However the traveler made the ascent of the river, he had to walk or
ride a mule from the Chagres across the low continental divide to the
city of Panama. If he left the river at Gorgona, the land trip was twenty-
six miles long, and if he went on to Cruces he had twenty-two miles of
trail still to cover. The Gorgona road was easier and better to travel in
dry season, but being unpaved was impassible in wet weather. The old
Spanish treasure trail passed through Cruces, and although it was in
ruinous shape, there was enough paving left to make it usable at all
seasons.

Osborne, in 1846, described the inhabitants of Gorgona and Cruces
as kindly and hospitable, and ready to give travelers all the accommodations they possessed for a trifling charge.[26] The towns kept their good
reputation, and Autenrieth spoke of two or three passable hotels at both
Gorgona and Cruces.[27] Although these towns were situated at a low elevation, they were often cooler and more comfortable than Chagres or
Panama.

For the land journey, the Argonaut hired a mule or walked, and either
made arrangements with a shipping company to transport his baggage
to Panama or bargained directly with a native muleteer or porter. If he
took the latter course, it was wise to take the man to the alcalde to have
him identified and vouched for as reliable. Even then it was a good plan
to draw up a formal contract for the transportation of the baggage, and
to make sure that it was actually started for Panama in advance of its

[24] New York *Herald,* March 30, 31, July 28, September 28, 1849; July 16, August 23, October
29, December 15, 1850; August 7, 1851; Panama *Echo,* March 16, 1850; Panama *Star,* September 13, October 18, 1850; February 11, March 14, 1851; Autenrieth, *Guide* [p. 17].

[25] New York *Herald,* August 23, October 29, 1850.

[26] Osborne, *Guide,* 257.

[27] Autenrieth, *Guide,* 9, 11.

owner. After taking all these precautions, the wise Argonaut still made it a point to keep his baggage actually in sight throughout the trip across the isthmus.[28]

Like everything else, the price of travel from the river to Panama fluctuated with demand. In 1846 a saddle mule was $5.00 and a luggage mule $3.00. The cost of a saddle mule had gone up to $10.00 by 1849, and in 1850 and 1851 the rate for a mule carrying one person with one trunk and one bag ranged from $15.00 to $30.00, with additional baggage $5.00 to $10.00 a hundred pounds.[29] Thus, the whole cost of the trip across the isthmus, which was about $18.00 in 1846, might be as much as $40.00 in 1850 for travel alone, with food and lodging in addition.

The land trip could be made in a day on muleback, or in two days afoot. The trails led through rolling hills, elevated plateaus, and jungle-filled valleys before emerging on the plain where the city of Panama stood. Due to long use, neglect, and erosion, there were gullies thirty feet deep in some parts of the Cruces road. They were not more than three feet wide at the bottom, and as two mules could not pass in them, the muleteers called out loudly before entering to make sure of meeting no one. Along the trails were occasional huts and ranchos, some of which provided food and lodging of a sort, although most travelers pushed on to Panama with all possible speed at this stage of the trip.[30]

On arrival at the city of Panama, the Argonaut gathered his baggage together, sought out lodgings, and made inquiry as to when the next vessel was leaving for San Francisco. Panama had a population of about 10,000 in 1849, and its sightly position on a peninsula jutting into the bay, its massive walls, and its air of antiquity were novel and impressive sights to the California-bound travelers. There were a few hotels in Panama before the gold rush. Their number multiplied and they took on American ways as the city became filled with emigrants, many of whom had to wait for weeks or months before obtaining passage north. In the fall of 1849 the Panama *Star* advertised the American Hotel, the French Hotel, and the Oregon Hotel, as well as bars and restaurants bearing names equally indicative of the Yankee invasion.[31]

The bottleneck of the isthmian route was at Panama. With many more vessels landing passengers at Chagres than there were to take them away

[28] Autenrieth, *Guide*, 9; Gregory, *Guide*, 5.

[29] Osborne, *Guide*, 260; Disturnell, *The Emigrant's Guide*, 40; New York *Herald*, March 31, 1849; Panama *Star*, February 11, 1851.

[30] Autenrieth, *Guide*, 12–13.

[31] Panama *Star*, November 10, 1849.

from Panama, there were often large backlogs awaiting transportation. The Pacific Mail had originally built three steamers for the Pacific coast service. The first of these, the *California,* sailed from Panama on her first voyage to San Francisco on January 31, 1849. These pioneer vessels were followed by others, but it took time to equip steamers and send them off around the Horn to the Pacific. By the beginning of 1851 there were 13 steamers in the Panama–San Francisco trade, but their combined carrying capacity was only 3,500, as compared with 5,000 on the Atlantic steamers at the same time. Added to this disparity of numbers was the fact that while a steamer on the New York–Chagres run could make a round trip in about a month, at least twice that much time elapsed between the trips of vessels on the Pacific coast owing to the greater distances.[32]

To augment the steamers, sailing vessels were pressed into service whenever possible. During the first six months of 1849, at least 27 sailing vessels—ships, barks, brigs, and schooners—sailed from Panama for San Francisco, carrying altogether about 3,500 passengers. Some were whalers, some were colliers, and some were local coasters, but they all were attracted by the high rates prevailing to turn themselves into temporary passenger carriers.[33] The voyage from Panama to San Francisco under sail was long and tedious, involving a reach out into the Pacific to the longitude of the Hawaiian Islands in order to meet winds favorable for the run back to the California coast. Therefore as soon as there were enough steamers on the Pacific to carry the traffic, sailing vessels disappeared from the Panama–San Francisco passenger trade.

Passenger accommodations were inadequate and there were still periods of serious congestion at Panama, though everything which would sail was pressed into service. When the *California* sailed northward on her first voyage, more than 700 people sought passage in her, and although she was crowded to the utmost, she left more than half of them behind.[34] By mid-April, 1849, more than 3,000 were at Panama awaiting transportation; but enough sailing vessels appeared to take them all within a month.[35] At the end of December that year there were 2,700 emigrants on the isthmus, while the ships immediately available to carry

---

[32] Steamers in service at the beginning of 1851 were: *Antelope, California, Carolina, Columbus, Isthmus, New Orleans, Northerner, Oregon, Panama, Republic, Sarah Sands, Tennessee,* and *Union.*

[33] New York *Herald,* February 16, 18, March 25, April 8, 10, May 10, 12, 17, 1849.

[34] *Ibid.,* March 4, 1849; Victor M. Berthold, *The Pioneer Steamer "California," 1848–1849* (Boston and New York, 1932), 37–42, 47–50.

[35] New York *Herald,* May 10, 17, 1849.

them would not accommodate more than 500.[36] So it went, until early in 1851, when there were enough steamers to take care of the demand, and crowds ceased to accumulate as in the earlier days.[37]

Wise travelers bought through tickets for the trip before leaving the United States and were thereby assured of accommodations on Pacific steamers. Many, however, arrived at the isthmus with no tickets from there to San Francisco, and depended on luck to obtain the desired accommodations on the spot. They were patrons of the ticket exchanges in Panama, which did a lively business "upon the Wall Street plan" in buying and selling California tickets.[38] Competition between steamship lines and fluctuations in demand for space increased the uncertainty of this business and the variations in prices of tickets from day to day.

When delays were long, grumbling and public meetings were the chief outlets for the impatience of the emigrants. At least one near-riot directed at the Pacific Mail agency in Panama was halted only by the timely arrival of a long-expected steamer.[39] Ill-feeling engendered by boredom, impatience, and the hot weather also helped stir up trouble between the emigrants and the Panamanians. In May, 1850, there was a bad riot in Panama which started in a quarrel between an American and a native and ended with several dead on both sides. The local constabulary was often unable to keep order on the isthmus, and the United States consuls at Panama and Chagres repeatedly urged that naval vessels be stationed at both ports.[40]

Another source of irritation among the Argonauts was the landing tax charged by the local government. Though it was only $2.00, there were repeated objections and refusals to pay until it went out of force.[41]

Another reason for impatience on the isthmus was its notoriously unhealthful climate. Although there are no statistics on mortality among the Argonauts, the diaries and reminiscences of the time bear witness that a considerable number died on the isthmus. Malaria was the only endemic and common disease, and the frequently mentioned "Panama fever" was probably a form of this. It was seldom fatal. But there were cholera epidemics at Panama in 1849 and 1850, and these were responsible for most of the deaths among the emigrants.[42]

---

[36] *Ibid.*, December 8, 1849.
[37] Henry Tracy to M. O. Roberts, Panama, March 9, 1851, *Heilman* vs. *Roberts,* 271.
[38] New York *Herald,* February 16, 18, April 10, May 10, June 26, 1849; May 25, 1850.
[39] *Ibid.*, October 14, 1849; Panama *Echo,* March 16, 1850; Panama *Star,* March 17, 1849.
[40] New York *Herald,* June 6, 1850; Index, Dispatches, 248, 302, 366–367.
[41] Panama *Star and Herald,* January 3, 1857.
[42] *Ibid.*, September 10, 1868.

Like the landing at Chagres, the embarkation at Panama had to be made in small boats, since the tidal flats on the sea side of the city kept large steamers from coming in close. At first, passengers were carried on the backs of natives from the beach to waiting boats in which they were rowed, paddled, or sailed out to the waiting steamer. By 1850 the Pacific Mail had a steam tender in service, which greatly facilitated embarkation.[43]

Once aboard the steamer, there remained a voyage of about three weeks to San Francisco, punctuated by one or more calls at Mexican ports to replenish the coal supply. Thus, the journey from New York to San Francisco by way of Panama took at least six weeks in the gold rush period, and if connections did not work out as planned, or ships were scarce at Panama, it sometimes took much longer. At that, the Panama route offered a good chance of getting to California faster than by any other way.[44]

The Argonaut who chose to go by Panama faced hardships and some real dangers. He ran the risk of a long delay at the isthmus. His trip was seldom a cheap one, and it might be very costly if he had to wait for a ship or suffered illness. On the other hand, it offered the possibility of quicker arrival in California than any other route. It had variety and interest. As travel increased and the isthmian crossing became better organized, the Panama route developed into the surest and most comfortable, as well as the fastest, means of travel to California.

[43] Gregory, *Guide,* 6; Panama *Star,* September 13, November 15, 1850.

[44] After the advent of faster steamers and the completion of the Panama Railroad in 1855, the Panama journey could be made in about three weeks.

South American Ports of Call

OSCAR LEWIS

[Oscar Lewis of San Francisco is a prolific writer on the West. His titles include *The Big Four* (New York, 1938) and *The Silver Kings* (New York, 1948). His next book, *Sea Routes to the Gold Fields,* will include this paper, in somewhat different form.]

IN 1849, the voyage from east coast ports of the United States to San Francisco, via Cape Horn, was so long that almost all the gold rush ships had to make at least two intermediate stops to replenish supplies of food and water and to make needed repairs. The favorite ports of call were Rio de Janeiro, below the great bulge of Brazil, and Valparaiso, about midway on the long coastline of Chile. These, however, were by no means the only stopping places. Some ships put in at Havana, but that was mainly to take on cargoes of sugar, molasses, or rum, which the owners, or the trading companies that had the crafts under charter, hoped to sell profitably in California.

Most Argonauts made their first contact with foreign soil in Brazil, either at Rio or on the island of St. Catherine's, several hundred miles farther south. Many skippers preferred St. Catherine's, which had long been a stopping place for American whalers, and which had a good harbor, excellent water, and ample supplies of wood and fruit. Moreover, it was less frequented than Rio and so promised less delay than was likely to be encountered in that crowded harbor. Finally, and perhaps most important, government regulations were laxly enforced on the island, and a foreign ship which offered proper inducements to the port officials was often required to pay far less in harbor fees than it would have had to pay at Rio.

After five or six weeks at sea, the northerners commonly found their first sight of this tropical island picturesque in the extreme. "St. Catherine's," wrote Richard Hale from the deck of the *General Worth,* "presents a very lovely picture ... its high, peaked rocks, its tree-covered mountains ... make a beautiful vista from the deck of the brig.... The surrounding views of scattered isles dotting the blue waters, with nestling villages of shining white houses on the crescent shaped shores ... paint a scene long to be remembered—a paradisian hiding place."

Close acquaintance, however, usually tempered the enthusiasm of the newcomers. The town was small, with little to offer in the way of amusement. The houses that had appeared so picturesque when viewed across an expanse of blue water proved to be ramshackle adobes, over-crowded, squalid, and evil-smelling. The inhabitants—Spaniards, Portuguese, Negroes, or a mixture of all three—seemed to the brisk northerners a deplorably unenterprising lot. They were not long discovering, however, that these unprepossessing natives were crafty traders. The appearance of a ship in the roadstead was a signal for a numerous crew of peddlers, "swarthy, fierce-looking men in huge straw hats and not much else," to put off from the beaches in small boats, converging on the newcomer like a fleet of pirates. Their frail crafts were loaded high with oranges, bananas, limes, plantains, guavas, and other exotic fruits, which they proceeded to offer at extremely high prices. Later, the first keen edge taken off their appetites, the Yankee visitors regained their bargaining instinct, and this, aided by competition among the rival peddlers, sent prices tumbling. One prudent New Englander, who delayed making his purchases during the first ten minutes of trading, ended by buying a basket containing a hundred large oranges for the equivalent of ten cents. His more impetuous fellows had paid a like sum for a mere half dozen.

At the height of the California rush, St. Catherine's was overrun with Yankees. When the *Cantero* dropped anchor in December, 1849, there were eleven other ships in the harbor, all flying the American flag and all but two bound for the gold fields. Small boats shuttled between the ships and the beach, loaded with young men who, after weeks of confinement, were avid for excitement. Naïve and curious, they engulfed the town, crowded the stores and bars and restaurants, and took long tramps into the country, where they marveled at the rank tropical growth, so different from the austere hills of home. Of course they found little of which they approved. Having observed the inhabitants at their work and play, with characteristic Yankee brashness they concluded that this indolent race could teach them nothing. The narrow streets were in bad repair and littered with rubbish, and in the country the roads were little more than trails. There were few wagons and fewer carriages; some rode horseback, but the majority walked; and most goods were carried by slaves. The northerners were fascinated by the enormous loads these stalwart blacks supported as they swung along the wooded trails of the back country, and by the Negro women who moved with unconcern through the crowded streets with heavily laden trays, three feet wide, balanced on their heads. The houses had no glass in their windows, a gate served for a door, and few of the rooms had wooden floors.

But if the natives struck the Yankees as lax and unenterprising, nature herself was prodigal. Benjamin Dore, fresh from the stony, uncoöperative fields of his native Maine, wrote in his diary:

Every thing groes . . . pine apples orenges lemons . . . peaches figs bananers water melons onions sweet potatoes rice cofee corn cucumbers potatoes &c., with but little cultivation   they live very easy but [with] avery little . . . enterprize about them aman that is worth four or five thousand dollars is thought to be very rich. . . . all most one half of [the] people is blacks.

In general, the visitors were well behaved, but their delight at finding themselves on land, in a country foreign to anything they had experienced, was such that their exuberance sometimes got out of hand. Dore, in December, 1849, back on the *Cantero* after an evening ashore, wrote:

In the evening 2 boat loads of us went on shore withe musick   called to an inglishmans house and stoped afew moments   from there we marched about 1 mile down the shore to aplace called the widows where found sever[al] boats crews dancing and runing around on the beach . . . it was a place for refreshments and mareners home.

A few nights later, after putting up at a tavern "called the germun house," Dore "retired to rest" at ten but "was waked . . . by the singing and holering of the yankeys for there was agreat many of them in the city."

Not all the noise was due to simple high spirits. The shops purveyed a cheap and potent aguardiente, "two drinks of which sufficed to paralyze the unwary," and drunkenness among the emigrants was reported by most diarists. When there were clashes between the Yankees and the natives, alcohol was usually responsible. Another source of friction was the visitors' ignorance of the customs of the country and their habit of regarding as reprehensible whatever differed from the usages at home. Much was written of the Latin American's habit of naming an exorbitant price for whatever he had to sell, in the expectation that the buyer would make his offer correspondingly low, with the deal being consummated after a long and mutually agreeable period of haggling. Unacquainted with this tradition, the northerner either paid the asking price or else stalked out of the shop; in either case he was convinced that South American merchants were all unprincipled rascals.

Not St. Catherine's but Rio was the first port of call for most gold rush ships. Landing at Rio was attended by far more formality than at the smaller port. No one was allowed to board an incoming ship or to leave her until she had passed inspection by two groups of Brazilian officials, representing the board of health and the customs service. But once

these examinations were over, the bars were let down and a waiting fleet
of small boats drew alongside. Soon the deck was crowded with visitors,
all on urgent business: peddlers, men with small boats to hire, reporters
for Rio newspapers seeking details of the voyage and news of the outer
world, agents for local business houses, many of them American owned,
soliciting trade and offering advice—which was not always disinterested—
on what shops, hotels, and restaurants to patronize.

A large city even in gold rush times, Rio was not overrun with the
California emigrants as were smaller South American ports. But the gold
hunters were numerous enough, and noisy enough, to make their presence felt. In the first three months of 1849, eighty-six California-bound
ships put into the harbor; sometimes a dozen arrived in a single day,
bearing as many as a thousand passengers. "A large number, you think,"
commented John Linville Hall, the historian of the *Henry Lee,* "to pour
into the streets of a town in a single day. Yet the number were nothing
in so populous a city as Rio, if the persons in question were orderly dis-
posed." It was not how numerous the North American visitors were,
Hall thought, but their bad manners, that made them conspicuous.

We know they had been in a high and unnatural state of excitement before
leaving home [Hall continued] . . . and making due allowance also for the
natural ebullition of spirits on coming to port; yet . . . there is still left a score
of riot, excess, and rowdyism to be acknowledged which ill beseems the American character. Many a Californian has had the pleasure of passing a night in
the Calaboose in payment of trenching on the public quiet. Some, for crimes
of a more serious nature, had been sentenced to the Penitentiary for a term
of years.

In Hall's view, the visitors made a sorry showing as compared to the
Brazilians. "Not a citizen or a slave did we see intoxicated, or any way
riotous during the week's time we were in port; on the contrary, the
inhabitants seemed quietly attentive to their own business—courteous to
their foreign guests—and, indeed, wonderfully forbearing of their
follies,"

The Yankees, in general, were favorably impressed with Rio, and even
those whose exuberance got them into trouble had praise for the hos-
pitality of the citizens. Public buildings, churches, and gardens were
opened to them, and the visitors found many of these superior to those
at home. To the northerners the climate, "seldom very hot or very dry,
never cold," seemed ideal, and the variety and beauty of the flowers and
shrubs aroused their unstinted admiration.

But unalloyed praise was not habitual to the strongly nationalistic visitors, and having paid tribute to the courtesy of the Brazilians and the natural beauty of Rio's setting, the diarists proceeded with gusto to expose the other side of the shield. Hall, having devoted several paragraphs to praising the city's parks and private gardens, added:

While we readily concede that the taste and skill of the Brazilians exceed ours in this particular department, yet, in respect to all the great purposes of life, we must think the scale is decidedly in our favor. Nay, we go farther; we believe that in agriculture, commerce, and invention, indeed in every branch of useful industry, they are, at least, fifty years behind the age.

Even more critical of Brazil and the Brazilians was L. M. Schaeffer, who, fresh from a Maryland farm, reached Rio in 1849 on the *Flavius*. His unfavorable impressions began even before he touched land. The native boatmen, he observed, did not know how to handle their oars, and the crowd gathered at the dock seemed to him "a trifling set of beings." Schaeffer went to a hotel: he found its accommodations miserable. The Emperor's chapel stood near by—it did "not compare with the Baltimore Exchange." Whatever he saw merely confirmed his conviction that all things were ordered better in Yankeeland. The houses had no proper cellars, the gutters were in the middle of the streets (obviously the wrong place for them), and the streets themselves "need very much the attention of the street sweeper." Water for household use was drawn from public wells, and on a visit to the navy yard he found work on a warship proceeding so slowly that he was moved to suppose, "by the time it was finished, the wood would be pretty much decayed." He granted that the central market was large and reasonably clean, but the meat looked to him like horseflesh, and he thought it inexpertly cut. "They want a Yankee butcher among them." Schaeffer returned to the *Flavius*, rejoicing at the privilege of again "treading the deck of our American vessel," the perfect symbol of rampant Americanism.

The stay in Rio commonly lasted about a week. As the time for sailing drew near, passengers busied themselves laying in supplies of fresh fruit, wine, and other products designed to fortify them against the trials and hazards of the Cape Horn passage. On the final night in port all stayed late on shore to celebrate their last contacts with urban life for many weeks. These farewell revels sometimes got the Argonauts into trouble. The hour of sailing was fixed to take advantage of the outgoing tide, and those who were not on board at the specified time were unceremoniously left behind. To be stranded in a foreign city with all one's friends and possessions standing out to sea was of course an unenviable situation, even though the victims had only themselves to blame. But some found themselves thus abandoned through no fault of their own. Unprincipled skippers were not averse to slipping away before the announced time, knowing that fewer mouths to feed would favorably affect the profits of the voyage, and knowing too that at the next port of call other passengers would be clamoring to be taken on board and willing to pay well for the privilege. Thus, at Rio and elsewhere, was left stranded "many an unwary passenger, who, without money or baggage, is left to such comfort ashore as the gloomy circumstances may afterwards unfold."

For all the emigrants' impatience to reach the gold fields, it was observed that while many begrudged the time spent at Rio or St. Catherine's, all welcomed with delight the prospect of a second stop, this time on the Pacific side of the continent. This was mainly because the second leg of their voyage had included the tedious passage round Cape Horn, and the knowledge that that ordeal was safely behind them put entire ships' companies in a mood for celebration as they headed north toward Talcahuano or Valparaiso. The first of these ports lay some three hundred miles south of Valparaiso; its harbor was adequate and its setting picturesque, surrounded by high hills covered with thick forests. These last were a welcome sight after the snowy desolation farther south. "Some of the trees have a shade of light green, reminding us of fields of wheat in Maine," wrote Joseph Lamson, whose ship, the *James W. Paige,* dropped anchor there in July, 1849. The town itself, at the head of a long bay, seemed from a distance a spot of extraordinary attraction, its white walls and tiled roofs rising steeply from the water's edge. But here again a closer view brought disillusion. "Judge then of my disappointment," wrote Lamson, "when on landing I found myself in the most filthy and disgusting village I ever beheld."

Talcahuano, in short, was typical of most remote seaport towns in the middle of the last century. A curious combination of primitive outpost and cosmopolitan trading center, it had both the vigor and vices of the frontier. Most residents lived in "little huts made of stakes driven into the ground, interwoven with twigs, and plastered over with mud," yet the bay shore was lined with substantial business houses, their storerooms piled high with the products of the country awaiting export and with goods brought in from the world's trading centers. The owners or managers of these businesses—mostly foreigners, many of them Americans—lived in large and comfortable houses on the hillsides above.

By the middle of 1849 the heavy California traffic had already given the town a distinctly American appearance. Those newly arrived were impressed by a profusion of signs designed to attract the custom of the Yankees. During a short walk on the water front one visitor saw the California Hotel, the American Hotel, American House, New Bedford House, New York Restaurant, Eagle Hotel, and others. Some of these establishments had been in existence before the gold rush began, for Talcahuano had long been a port of call for the American whalers. Hotels and restaurants were numerous, and bars even more so. The strong wines of Chile and its aguardiente were both plentiful and cheap, and those newly ashore proved avid customers. As in most seaport towns of the period, prostitution was a flourishing industry, although the conventions of that mid-Victorian era were so strong that few of the diaries contain any hint that the Yankees patronized such establishments. One finds instead—and that but rarely—only such oblique references as this, from Lamson's journal:

As I passed into the cross streets I saw a great many women seated or standing at their doors. . . . Many of them were very filthy, though some were neatly dressed, and were rather pretty. They had dark complexions, fresh, florid cheeks, bright, black eyes, and black, glossy hair hanging down their backs. . . . They had a smile and a word for all strangers, but their smiles were those of the siren.

Valparaiso, a more imposing place than Talcahuano, although its harbor was less good, was the favorite west coast port of call; more gold ships stopped there than at any South American port except Rio. The northerners found its setting extremely picturesque; one Argonaut described it as being "as theatrical as a stage setting," adding: "A spur from the Andes shoots out to the coast and ends on a promentory. . . . The debris from this spur has formed a low and narrow strip of ground where stands the city." Unlike most South American cities, Valparaiso's streets were wide and straight, "as wide as Washington Street in Boston." The leading business firms were handsomely housed and, as at Talcahuano, rows of pretentious residences were perched high on the cliffside. Valparaiso was a seaport and as such had its full share of "sailors' boarding houses, brothels and grog shops," although this quarter was more picturesquely situated than elsewhere.

Rising abruptly above the southern end of the city [wrote T. R. Warren, early in 1849] are three conical hills . . . named respectively the "Fore, Main and Mizzen Tops"—their terraced sides occupied by sailors' boarding-houses and gambling-hells of the very lowest description. Here jack retires on the receipt of his wages, from whence, after being stupified with bad liquor and beaten and robbed of his money, he is summarily ejected, lucky not to be sent headlong down one of the steep precipices, as many a poor devil has been before him.

The huge traffic set in motion by the gold discovery had, of course, a marked effect on a dozen seaports on both sides of the continent. Captain George Coffin, whose ship, the *Alhambra*, arrived in August, 1849, recorded its impact:

I found in Valparaiso several passenger ships bound to California, and the great number of Americans on shore . . . seemed to nationalize the town. Yankees did just as they pleased and the city authorities were powerless to restrain them; but the great California emigration has been a godsend to this place, and they can well put up with the Yankee dare-devil spirit for the sake of the Yankee gold. Everything in the line of provisions has advanced fifty per cent. In the staple article of flour California has opened a new and extensive demand, and hundreds of acres are now in wheat where last year was nothing but weeds and thistles.

Some four hundred miles due west of Valparaiso lies Juan Fernández, and to this remote island the gold rush brought for the first and last time in its history a period of brisk activity. Not more than fifty ships stopped there during 1849 and 1850, but these must have seemed a great armada to the island's handful of inhabitants, to whom the rare call of a whaler or the twice yearly visits of a supply ship from the mainland had theretofore been their only contacts with the outer world.

The California ships stopped there mainly because the island, although it was destitute of other supplies, had an abundance of wood, fruit, and water, the last flowing from cool mountain springs and carried in wooden flumes to the ocean's edge. While the crews refilled the ships' water casks, passengers explored the island, inspected the caves that had once sheltered Chile's hardened criminals in the days when Juan Fernández had been a penal colony, or gathered the fruit that grew prodigiously in the abandoned orchards. To most visitors, however, these were not Juan Fernández' main attractions; curiously, although the island was quite without commercial importance, it was better known to most Argonauts than any of the great cities of the mainland. The reason, of course, is that this was Robinson Crusoe's island, and the Defoe romance was one of the most widely read books of the day.

Typical of the spirit in which hundreds of young Americans approached this shrine, is that of twenty-two-year-old Richard Hale, whose ship, the *General Worth,* dropped anchor in the cove in March, 1849:

We are now getting into shape for port,—the most fascinating spot, to me, on the face of the globe! . . . What schoolboy . . . but has imagined himself cast-away on this very island . . . ? To-morrow I shall see the enchanted isle! Not the picture of fancy, but the real ground . . . perhaps see the cave that Robinson dug, or the ruins of his little hovel.

Such was the power of Defoe's story that few who stopped at Juan Fernández appear to have had any suspicion that Robinson Crusoe was other than an actual person. One Yankee, E. I. Barra, who arrived in mid-'forty-nine on the *Samson,* admits—rather grudgingly, it appears—that Crusoe was a fictional counterpart of Alexander Selkirk, but even he shrugs the matter off: the cave he reverently stands before is far more Crusoe's than Selkirk's. "The poor fellow!" wrote Barra. "I could almost picture him standing before me, with his unique garments of goat skins, looking with longing eyes out upon the broad expanse of the ocean, perchance to discover some friendly sail, that might be directed thitherward by a kind Providence." Perhaps it was these visitors' own close knowledge of the vast reaches of the sea that gave them a sense of kinship with Crusoe and an understanding of the realties of his dilemma.

Sometimes the first stops on the Pacific were at points farther north, either at Callao or at one of the islands of the Galapagos group. Those whose ships put in at Callao counted themselves fortunate, for Peru's chief city, Lima, lay only a few miles inland, and even a brief visit there opened the eyes of the northerners, giving them a new comprehension of that land's long history, its tradition of culture, and the magnificence and antiquity of its public monuments. Small wonder that the Yankees, after a day or two in this once rich and still vastly impressive capital, observing the well-ordered life of the inhabitants, the luxurious shops and varied amusements, returned to their cramped and austere little ships with a new respect for this ancient outpost of Spanish American civilization.

Northernmost of the stopping places on the Cape Horn route was a place quite different from Lima: the Galapagos Islands, lying astride the equator, some six hundred miles west of the mainland. Comparatively few put in at these barren and rocky islands, but those who did found much of interest to record in their diaries or sketchbooks. The *Canton* dropped anchor off Chatham, one of the easternmost of the group, in

August, 1849, and Joseph Kendall thus pictured it in a letter to his young daughter in New York:

A description of this island will seem to you singular in the extreme. It is without any water, with the exception of one place about eight miles from where we lay anchored. The greater part of the island is utterly scorched with the sun. . . . It is all of volcanic matter, like burnt black clinkers, which rattle like a bell at every step one takes. Not a blade of grass is to be seen, but there are some very beautiful shrubs, with aromatic scents, very cheering to my senses.

Although there was a lack of vegetation over much of the islands, Kendall—like many later visitors, including Charles Darwin—was impressed by the abundance of land and marine life. In particular he was charmed by the vast number of birds, large and small and of many species, and all quite without fear. The chief novelty to the Yankees, however, were the huge colonies of turtles for which the islands were famous, and which the newly arrived welcomed as a means of adding variety to a diet that had grown excessively monotonous. There were two varieties, land and sea turtles, both so large that two men could lift one with difficulty, and—like the birds—they showed no fear of humans, whom they permitted to approach with complete unconcern. The *Canton* group gathered specimens of both varieties and during their stay enjoyed turtle soup and turtle steak three times a day. When the craft set sail again her deck was crowded with sixty of the great creatures, destined to disappear one by one into the kettles of the galley during the long cruise to San Francisco.

The Clampers

CARL I. WHEAT

[The author, who—with George Ezra Dane and Leon Whitsell—was one of the "re-vivers" of *E Clampus Vitus,* is past N.G.H. of Yerba Buena and Platrix Chapters, Honorary N.G.H. of Skunks Misery Chapter, and Founder of Little Hatchet Chapter on the banks of the turbid Potomac.]

IT WAS EARLY in the 'fifties that "The Ancient and Honorable Order of E Clampus Vitus" first appeared on the California scene. The time was one of vast upheaval, human as well as physical. And after a hard day in the dirt and muck of some Sierra diggin's, where else but in the Clampers' "Hall of Comparative Ovations" could a man rediscover those values that seemed otherwise so lacking in the hard life of the California canyons?

E Clampus Vitus spread like wildfire through the mountains. Few, indeed, were the camps where the order's great horn—the "Hewgag"—did not on occasion hoarsely bray. Surely, the succinct Constitution of the Order displayed its roisterous spirit as could nothing else.

"Article One," read that unorthodox document: "All members are Officers."

"Article Two," it eloquently continued: "All Officers are of equal in-dignity."

That was all. But it was enough. When the Hewgag blew, the brethren gathered from far and near. It was a signal that a sucker had appeared in camp—some "Poor Blind Candidate" ripe for a new experience. For the only ritual of this significant organization of gold rush days was that of initiation, and the only stated meeting was before or after the full moon when such a one should come upon the scene ready for immolation on the altar of merriment.

On those gala occasions when—in the vociferous spirit of the mid-nineteenth-century Yankee—a parade was to be staged along the camp's lone street, it was usually the Clampers who stole the show, marching be-hind a stalwart soul carrying a pole that bore a hoop skirt with the strange device, "This Is the Banner We Fight Under." Nor was it only in con-nection with such celebrations that the Clampers shone, for were they not brethren ready at the merest hint of their mysterious Sign of Distress to come to one another's assistance, and did not their well-known sign of recognition—the Sign of the Well Jackass—betoken a vitality that even the drab life of the diggin's could not destroy?

"All for one and one for all" could, indeed, have been the motto of this lusty Order. As a matter of fact, however, the Order's hortatory watchword was: "For the benefit of widows and orphans—but more especially of widows!" And when a brother, worn by toil and broken in the search for gold, could no longer carry on, the brethren, one and all, would come to his assistance. It is said that fifteen dollars a month from the Clampers would keep a miner in bacon and flour, beans, and saleratus, and that in those better days E Clampus Vitus had but two rules to guide its members in their eleemosynary roles:

(1) A man shall come in person to the Hall of Comparative Ovations for this helpful dole; and

(2) Payments shall commence two years after death.

When, in the late 'twenties of this softer century, a band of latter-day enthusiasts sought once more to capture the spirit of the Order's elder days, it was found that little in the way of written data could be found to describe and explain those small and intimate details of the past that at such times bear so great significance. It was the late lamented Ezra Dane who suggested the answer. "During those early days," said he, "no Clamper in attendance at a stated meeting was ever in any condition to take minutes of the ceremonies." And, he would add, "After the meeting had concluded no one could be found who could remember what had happened."

The Grand Lodge of the Order convened at Mokelumne Hill, but from the far north of Downieville and Sierra City to the southernmost diggin's, even beyond Mariposa, chapters of E Clampus Vitus flourished. Let no benighted individual place a period after that fateful "E" (as was done—ignominiously—in a recently celebrated catalogue of Californiana), and let no person of whatever race, color, or previous condition succumb to the heretical placing of an "s" after the "p" of Clampus.

The actual revival of the Order began at Yerba Buena early in the 'thirties, and by a happy circumstance there came to the group a voice from the past in the person of Adam Lee Moore, last Noble Grand Humbug of the Order in that earlier Dispensation. Before he passed from the scene a few years ago at the ripe age of ninety and nine, he—the *Clampatriarch* of the revival—brought to these younger and later Clampers not only a Charter of Apostolic Succession but a youthful spirit that pervaded many a Pilgrimage to the Diggin's with mirth and lusty human wisdom. Soon another chapter was erected in the Queen of the Cow Counties, far to the south, and others later were convened at Camptonville, Nevada City, Auburn, Hangtown, Columbia, Murphy's Camp, Skunks Misery, and other memorable spots. The New Dispensation carries on, often incredulous of the tales it hears of the Clampers of old.

In *The Enigmatical Book of Vitus* the story of the resuscitation of the Order has been told, and the spirit of *Credo quia absurdum* has been outlined in *The Curious Book of Clampus*. Later, *The Esoteric Book of E* and *Ye Preposterous Booke of Brasse* carried the tale farther. The literature of the revival grows apace.

Once each year the brethren gather at Yerba Buena on a night nigh unto the twenty-fourth of January, when their lamented one-time Clampatriarch, James W. Marshall, turns over in his grave three times in their favor. Once, also, in each year, "before or after the Full Moon," they devote themselves to a pilgrimage to some spot hallowed by the picks and pans of forty-niner days, there to imbibe by some obscure but revivifying osmosis the spirit of the elder days.

E Clampus Vitus was a force of no little significance in those earlier decades. It represented release from toil—respite from sweat—a chance to laugh with and at one's fellows. And so, when the sonorous echoes of the Hewgag resounded through the Sierra silences, few there were who did not drop their picks and haste them to the Great Hall, where amid Comparative Ovations and mighty mirth "Poor Blind Candidates" were brought out and instructed in the mysteries of the Order. To the query "What say the Brethren?" the assembled Clampers would shout "Satisfactory!" and the Grand Noble Recorder would reply, with august dignity, "And so recorded."

What is the significance of the mystic words which designate the Order? What can "E" or "Clampus," or even "Vitus," mean in this connection? That is a secret the answer to which reposes only in the astral memories of Clampers long since gone to their reward. It is, in fact, the only true secret still recorded and remembered by the Order, for no member now in good standing knows the answer. An odd situation? Yes, but wholly in keeping with those other factors which render this agreeable fraternity of the gold days memorable and worthy of perpetuation.

The California Clippers

RAYMOND A. RYDELL

[Raymond A. Rydell is assistant professor of history in Los Angeles State College. This paper is part of a larger study on The Cape Horn Route to the Pacific.]

THE DECADE of the 'fifties was the Golden Age of the American merchant marine. Towering clippers for a time carried the bulk of the premium high-sea commerce of the world, including the California trade between the east and west coasts of the United States by way of Cape Horn.

During these years, the more proficient utilization of the interocean highway was in marked contrast to the rule-of-thumb navigation which preceded the 'fifties. Before the first publication of the findings of Lieutenant Matthew Fontaine Maury, scientific navigation of the route was almost unknown. Vessels making the passage in anything less than 200 days were thought to have made a fair voyage. It is not difficult to understand why. Most sailing masters thought of the voyage as a personal war between themselves and the winds and currents, in the course of which it was mandatory for them to strive each day to move as much closer to their goal—and along as straight a line—as was humanly possible. The result was that they wasted precious time beating against head winds or running before favorable breezes into areas of calms, when they should have considered the voyage as an integrated whole and striven to avoid, or to work around such obstacles, or to use them to better final advantage.[1]

Once clear of Boston Light or Sandy Hook, the conventional Yankee skipper usually drove south-southwest along a great circle toward the equator, notwithstanding the fact that he might find the wind directly ahead, and would, as often as not, arrive off Cape St. Roque in an unfavorable position to weather it. After he had worked round this easternmost tip of South America he would move along the coast with reasonable assurance until he approached 50 degrees south latitude. From this point in the South Atlantic to 50 degrees south latitude in the Pacific each navigator was "on his own." Some stayed to the east of the Falkland Islands, some to the west. For those who chose the west side there remained the choice of either passing between Tierra del Fuego and Staten

---

[1] See the discussion in Matthew F. Maury, *Explanations and Sailing Directions, to Accompany the Wind and Current Charts* (7th ed., Philadelphia, 1855), 324 ff. This lengthy work includes many logs and tabulations of voyages in addition to charts and sailing instructions.

Island, through the Strait of Lemaire, or making a detour around them. Some might even attempt to negotiate Magellan's route, but few were willing to risk their vessels in the treacherous winds and tides of the strait. Off the Horn, a skipper would have to make sufficient westing to clear the cape as best he could. A few failed altogether, foundering in the heavy gales, putting back to Rio de Janeiro in distress, or standing off to the east to round the world in the other direction.[2] The others clawed their way west and pointed north for San Francisco or some intermediate point of call in the South Pacific.

The passage from off the northern coast of South America to the coast of California was the slowest of the entire voyage from New York or New England to the west coast. Some vessels consumed three months and more in beating up the coast to San Francisco and other California ports; it was not until Maury pointed the way and his recommendations were borne out by the fast passages of the early clippers that the time for this leg of the voyage was substantially reduced.

Maury's researches and directions revolutionized the navigation of the Cape Horn route. Yet the thorough investigations in ocean geography and meteorology upon which his conclusions were based were not his alone; the abstract logs which were his sources were faithfully completed at sea by coöperating masters, who sent enough of them to his Washington laboratory to enable him to construct a maritime mosaic of winds and currents from which better sea routes could be deduced.[3] The new routes materially helped to reduce the average time of a voyage to 133 days and to make possible the amazing ninety-day passages of the *Flying Cloud, Swordfish,* and *Andrew Jackson.*

The master of a California clipper who followed Maury's charts and instructions would point much farther east than was conventional so as to reach sooner a meridian near 65 degrees west, where there was a reasonably good chance of encountering favorable trade winds.[4] From here to Cape St. Roque his course was laid out in convenient squares, with several alternates to suit the expected wind variations and the sailing qualities of various types of vessels. He would then be in a more favorable position

[2] An extended account of a foundering and rescue off the Horn is in James T. Seaver, Journal of a Voyage from Boston to San Francisco in Ship *May Flower,* entry for May 30, 1859; this journal is in the New York Public Library.

[3] Maury, *op. cit.,* 182–211, describes the system. The abstract logs—more than 5,000 in number—are in the Marine Division, Weather Bureau, United States Department of Agriculture Archives, in the National Archives; they are analyzed in part in a mimeographed Descriptive List, and a card-index file.

[4] Maury, *op. cit.,* 329 ff., charts the first segments of the run down the Atlantic. The following paragraphs generalize upon his details.

to round Cape St. Roque without being adversely affected by the peculiar winds and the coastal current. Then, instead of following an inshore track along the coasts of Brazil and Argentina, he was warned to stand off far enough from the land to avoid the worst of the pampero weather moving east from the Plate River mouth, yet not so far as to make it difficult for him to reach the Strait of Lemaire before attempting to round the Horn. Maury advised:

The reason for this recommendation is this: After crossing the parallel of Tierra del Fuego, the difficulty is to get to the westward. Therefore, it is better to make westing on this side, when it is practicable, and where the weather is mild, than to put it off for the stormy latitudes, where it is more difficult.[5]

Once opposite "old Cape Stiff," where the prevailing westerlies come around the corner of the continent as winds come around a bluff point of land in a harbor, a Maury navigator would—if unable to make progress because of headwinds—move south rather than attempt to fight it out in the shadow of the Horn. For experience proved that in the region between the cape and several degrees farther south a number of distinctly different winds were likely to be encountered, some of which were bound to be more favorable to a westbound ship than a hard gale blowing from dead ahead.

As clippers stood north from the Horn they did not try to drive along the coast directly toward San Francisco but made as much westing with their northing as possible—always favoring the port tack—so as to work out from the coast the maximum distance without losing time in getting to the north.[6] This enabled them to move more quickly into the southeast trade-wind region of the Pacific and, at the same time, to put as much distance as was practicable between themselves and the sharply contrary winds blowing from the arid plains of the American Southwest and northern Mexico far out to sea. They calculated to cross the equator between 105 degrees and 125 degrees, depending upon the season of the year and the reliability of the trades, where they were in position to drive toward the Golden Gate by using the force of the desert winds to aid them on the last leg of their voyage.

Writing in 1855,[7] Maury believed it possible for an able vessel under canvas to make the run from New York to San Francisco in eighty-five days, but only with a combination of circumstances and a succession of

[5] *Ibid.,* 481.
[6] *Ibid.,* 674 ff.
[7] *Ibid.,* 687, and Plate XVIII. Maury of course made adequate allowance for weather and wind changes during the several seasons.

winds that might occur not more frequently than once a year. Inasmuch as this goal was persistently sought but never attained, it is significant that several runs of less than ninety days from San Francisco to New York were never celebrated as were the longer runs from east to west.[8] The reason for this, of course, was that the eastbound vessels had blowing over their sterns the same winds that blew against the bows of the westbound and, other things being equal, could be expected to enjoy a quicker passage. The voyage itself was also shorter for eastbound ships, for they could follow the great circle route from San Francisco to Cape Horn, round the cape without wasting time and miles searching for near-favorable winds, point up the coast of Argentina, and follow another great circle track from Cape St. Roque to New York. Moreover, eastbound vessels were seldom heavily laden; their sailing qualities were never compromised but could be exercised to best advantage.

The clippers were not an entirely new design. They already had appeared as a standard type before the discovery of gold in California.[9] They were at first somewhat smaller in size, and their design reflected a different commercial purpose, but otherwise they were much the same. The clippers were an evolutionary, rather than a revolutionary, development, in which the ideas and experiments of Captain Nathaniel B. Palmer, the inspiration of John W. Griffith, the architecture of Samuel H. Pook and William H. Webb, the imaginative craftsmanship of Donald McKay, and the contributions of countless others were combined with the commercial demands of the times to produce the best in sail.[10]

Though the clipper type existed in the late 'forties, it was not until 1849 that there was enough stimulus to push the clippers to their highest point of development. In that year the opportunities for profits in the California trade following the discovery of gold, and the equally attractive prospects in the China-England tea trade following the final repeal

---

[8] Carl C. Cutler, *Greyhounds of the Sea: The Story of the American Clipper Ship* (New York, 1930), Appendix II, lists all the record passages.

[9] *United States Nautical Magazine and Naval Journal*, VI (April, 1857–September, 1857), 52. (Cited hereafter as *U.S.J.*). Full discussions of their evolution are in Charles E. Park, "The Development of the Clipper Ship," American Antiquarian Society *Proceedings*, XXXIX (1929), Part 1, pp. 49–76; Alexander Laing, *Clipper Ship Men* (New York, 1945), *passim*; Samuel E. Morison, *The Maritime History of Massachusetts, 1783–1860* (Boston, 1921), chap. xxii; Arthur H. Clark, *The Clipper Ship Era* (New York, 1910), chaps. i–vii; Cutler, *op. cit.*, chaps. i–xv.

[10] Laing, *op. cit.*, 165. Palmer's contributions are described at length in John R. Spears, *Captain Nathaniel Brown Palmer* (New York, 1922); the work of Griffith, Pook, and Webb is recorded in various issues of the *United States Nautical Magazine and Naval Journal*, of which Griffith was the editor; McKay's career is extensively treated in Richard C. McKay, ed., *Donald McKay and the Ships He Built* (Boston, 1925).

of the Navigation Acts, combined to bring about a surge in American maritime industry such as had not been known since the Napoleonic wars and would not be felt again until the first World War. An era of ship-building was begun that temporarily placed the United States alongside Great Britain as the leading maritime nation of the world, though ship for ship the quality of the American merchant marine was even superior to the British.

The Cape Horn route to California was the only practicable means by which Atlantic-seaboard merchants could reach the fabulous market of San Francisco. It was also the most comfortable, and often the cheapest, manner of travel to the gold fields. At the beginning of the rush, there-fore, almost every available vessel capable of withstanding the rigors of a Cape Horn passage had been pressed into service to carry Argonauts to the Pacific Coast.[11] So many were utilized for this purpose and so many were deserted inside the Golden Gate that an acute shortage of American shipping resulted at the very time when ocean transportation facilities were at a premium. Moreover, those clippers still on the stocks were al-ready committed to the newly opened China tea trade. Their fortunate owners took advantage of the singular commercial situation to send their new vessels round the Horn with freight for the California market, thence to Hong Kong to load tea for London.

The *Sea Witch* and the *Samuel Russell* both cleared New York early in the spring of 1850 and, according to this pattern, sailed round the world via San Francisco, Canton, and London.[12] The former vessel set a new record for the New York to California passage by standing in through the Golden Gate ninety-seven days after dropping her pilot off Sandy Hook. The *Samuel Russell,* though not so fast, had a more prosperous voyage. Loaded until her scuppers were only a foot above water, she earned better than $70,000, enabling her owners to write off the entire cost of her construction.[13]

---

[11] Robert G. Albion, *The Rise of New York Port, 1815–1860* (New York, 1939), 356, analyzes the effects.

[12] Sketches of the "career" of every American clipper are in the Percy Chase Manuscripts in the Houghton Library, Harvard University; three folio volumes contain more than 200 sepa-rate notebooks and folders concerning individual vessels. The most complete published work on individual clippers is Octavius T. Howe and Frederick C. Matthews, *American Clipper Ships 1833–1858* (2 vols., Salem, 1926–1927) (Publication No. 13 of the Marine Research So-ciety); the vessels are arranged alphabetically by name. Similar—though shorter—treatments are Howard I. Chappelle, *The History of American Sailing Ships* (New York, 1935), and Helen La Grange, *Clipper Ships of America and Great Britain, 1833–1869* (New York, 1936); see also Cutler, *op. cit.,* and Clark, *op. cit.,* Appendixes.

[13] Spears, *op. cit.,* 201–203, describes the voyage and its profits.

The effect of these and similar voyages upon American maritime industry in general and upon ship designing and construction in particular was profound. John W. Griffith, in discussing the clipper *Staghound*, explained it this way:

For a long time it was held by mercantile opinion that fast vessels were not so profitable as duller sailers, carrying larger cargoes; but the rise of freights, consequent upon the discovery of gold, and the emigration to California, determined the argument in the favor of all ambitious ship-builders and merchants, and *clippers* became the watchword of commercial men all over New-England, and in New York.[14]

Speed was the quality most sought; after naval architects such as Griffith, Pook, and Webb, who had long desired to concentrate their efforts on vessels of better-sailing qualities, but who had been restrained by cautious shipowners, were given free rein to create the best their ingenuity could devise. For some three years—as long as the boom lasted—it was a shipbuilder's utopia. At first New York took the lead in clipper construction, since here only were both capital and shipyards. But during 1850 and 1851 most yards contracted to build ocean steamers. Inasmuch as steamer construction was more profitable than the building of sailing vessels, New York firms were not inclined to revert at the moment; thus, more and more, clippers came to be contracted for in Boston and other New England seaports.[15] The trend continued in this direction, New York becoming best known for steamships, and Boston rapidly assuming the lead in clipper construction. Yet most clipper ships were owned by New York firms and operated out of that port a good part of the time.[16]

The boom years of the clipper era were 1850–1853. Then freight rates were the highest, profits the heaviest, and most of the record passages took place. The older China clippers *Architect* and *Memnon*—first of their type to pass through the Golden Gate after the discovery of gold—were soon followed by the larger California clippers, ships of more than twice their tonnage, built during 1849 expressly for the trade with San Francisco. These sleek and powerful vessels embodied in their design and construction all the lessons American shipbuilders had learned since the Declaration of Independence. Their concave lines of entry and their fine lines aft were meant to slip them through the water with minimum resist-

---

[14] *U.S.J.*, II (April, 1855–September, 1855), 401–402.
[15] *Ibid.*, VI (April, 1857–September, 1857), 442, explains the developments in New York and New England.
[16] Albion, *op. cit.*, 358.

ance, to help them clip through the waves—hence the popular name.[17] They were, in fact, streamlined.

Their hulls were designed so as to permit the maximum amount of canvas aloft, and, most significantly, their rugged construction was predicated upon their being driven to the limit under the most formidable weather conditions. These material factors, added to the efficiency of Yankee captains, most of whom had learned their profession in the transatlantic packets or the China trade, and the availability of Maury's *Sailing Directions* and *Wind and Current Charts,* go far toward explaining the remarkable performances of American merchant vessels in the 'fifties.

With its $60.00 per ton rate for freight to California, 1850 witnessed the launching or laying down of a score of the most successful clippers, including the *Staghound, Challenge, Witch of the Wave, Sovereign of the Seas,* and *Flying Cloud.* Only a few of these, notably the *Staghound,* were completed in time to arrive off the Golden Gate before the year had expired.[18] But their owners reaped a golden harvest that spurred their competitors to heroic effort to clear their vessels for the Pacific Coast before supply should balance demand in the California market. Indeed, so many made the voyage in the first part of 1851 that the San Francisco market became glutted.[19] Yet the commerce remained lucrative until 1853.

Of all the passages made in 1851, none is as celebrated as the maiden voyage of McKay's *Flying Cloud.* Built specifically for the California trade, and commanded by Josiah P. Cressy, she was the last word in sail that season. She cleared New York at 2:00 P.M., June 2, carrying a full cargo of general merchandise for San Francisco.[20] Five hours later she dropped the pilot off Sandy Hook and pointed southeast in fine weather. Three days later she carried away her main and mizzen topgallant mast and main topsail yard off Cape Hatteras. Cressy sent up new spars during the next two days and kept driving, passing other ships which were laboring under reefed topsails while he was carrying full sail. She crossed the equator on June 26 and rounded Cape St. Roque the same day. July 10 found her off the Plate. The next day, Cressy wrote in the log:

Heavy Gales, Close Reefed Topsails split fore Staysail & Main Topmast Staysail at 1 p.m. Discovered Main Masthead Sprung (same time Brig in Company

---

[17] For a concise discussion of clipper characteristics, see Jonas Pendlebury and Martin D. Stevers, *Sea Lanes: Man's Conquest of the Ocean* (New York, 1935), 255. Cutler, *op. cit.,* Appendix VII, reprints the plans of many well-known clippers; all the books on clippers devote considerable space to design and sail plans.

[18] Hinton Rowan Helper, *The Land of Gold: Realty versus Fiction* (Baltimore, 1855), chap. xiv, contains an account of a passage of the *Staghound.*

[19] Morison, *op. cit.,* 338.

[20] Her complete log is reprinted in Cutler, *op. cit.,* Appendix V.

to leeward lost fore & Main topmast) sent down Royal & Topmast Yards & Booms off Lower & Topsail Yard to releave the mast, very turbulent sea Running Ship Laboring hard & shipping large quantities of Water over lee Rail. Middle & Latter parts hard Gales & Harder squalls. No observations.[21]

July 26 found the vessel five miles off Cape Horn; the next day Cressy pointed north. On July 31, off Valparaiso, the log shows that the ship, for a time, was going through the water at better than eighteen knots and that the official distance run that day was 374 nautical miles. The weather continued favorable for the remainder of the passage, and on August 31, at 7:00 A.M., the *Flying Cloud* took on a pilot near the Farallones. She let go her anchor at 11:30 A.M., off North Beach, San Francisco, 89 days, 21 hours from New York. This record stood until 1854, when she bettered it by thirteen hours, the permanent record from anchor to anchor.

While Cressy was driving down the South Atlantic, the New York clipper *Challenge,* commanded by Robert H. Waterman, cleared New York. Waterman hoped also for a 90-day run, but it was too late in the year; violent weather off Cape Horn delayed him at least a week. The best he could do was 109 days from anchor to anchor. It must have been a rough trip in every respect; Waterman crushed the skulls of two of the crew to save the life of his chief mate; and three other seamen fell from— or were shot off—a yardarm while fighting gales off Cape Horn.[22]

On her 1851 voyage, the *Sea Serpent,* Captain William Howland, carried a freight manifest ten feet long.[23] All her bills of lading show the same rate: $1.00 per cubic foot, with 5 per cent added for primage. On 1,304 tons of freight (the approximate tonnage of the vessel), total charges to the shippers were $54,528.36; the ship itself had cost considerably less to construct. Reading straight down her freight list, one finds:

36	grt. casks Brandy	4	Packages Hatchets
30	⅛ " ditto	1	Cask & Box Hardware
2	cases Mdze.	1	Box Axe Handles
28	" "	5	Bales Blankets & box Samples
24	dozin Shovels	15	Bbls Alchohol
10	Pkg Axes	13	Boxes Mdze
2	Boxes Adzes	200	Coils Rope
4	Broad Axes	15	Kegs Shot

Hardware, liquor, and food made up most of her cargo.

---

[21] *Ibid.,* 523. He was encountering one of the violent pamperos that frequently blow off the Argentine coast.

[22] Discussions of the affair are to be found in Cutler, *op. cit.,* 186–191; and Clarke, *op. cit.,* 181–189. Waterman was almost lynched by a vigilance committee when he arrived in San Francisco.

[23] All the commercial documents of her voyages are in the S. Griffitts Morgan Manuscripts, 1843–1863, Vol. XXIII, in the Baker Library, Harvard University.

In all, forty-eight clippers arrived in San Francisco in 1851, each realizing enough, or nearly enough, to pay for itself in one voyage. Some came back over the same route to New York; more sailed on to China and England before pointing home.

The flood of clipper launchings continued into 1852 and 1853, clearings from eastern ports for San Francisco increasing proportionately. Ninety-five clipper ships and 10 clipper barks sailed from Atlantic ports for the Pacific Coast in 1852, and 145 cleared in 1853.[24] The former year saw the outstanding passages of the *Swordfish* and the *Sovereign of the Seas*. Both might have bettered the time of the *Flying Cloud* had they experienced slightly more favorable weather conditions; as it was, the *Swordfish* let go her anchor before Telegraph Hill only 90 days and 18 hours out of New York.

The *Sovereign of the Seas,* a new vessel under the command of Lachlan McKay, Donald McKay's older brother, took 103 days to make the passage. Carrying 3,000 tons of general freight—worth almost $100,000 to her owners in shipping charges,—she sailed from New York, August 4; her crew included 104 officers and men, and her passenger register listed 21 names.[25] The voyage was vividly described by one of her crew:

We sailed . . . with a fine leading breeze, but during the night the wind changed ahead, and blew a gale. The noble ship, however, clawed off shore like a pilot boat. . . .

Next morning the wind favored us and we were soon under all sail close hauled, walking to the eastward at the rate of 15 miles an hour, and long before sunset we were out of sight of land. . . .

The first sixteen days out we encountered strong southerly winds and made only 600 miles southing. Twenty-seven days out we crossed the equator having worked almost every inch of the way, dead to windward. . . . When we reached the Falkland Islands we had tremendous S. W. gales, with a sea awful to look at, yet we carried a heavy press of sail [McKay was out to beat the *Flying Cloud's* record] and actually drove the ship through it, standing off and on every four hours. Hail, snow, and screamers were our companions day and night, but most nobly did the gallant ship behave. . . .

[Captain McKay] carried on sail so as to make it truly frightful to look aloft, and fairly beat his ship dead to windward against head gales and currents, from the Falkland Islands to Cape Horn. . . .

---

[24] The total number of one-way transits of the Horn by American vessels—including clippers—in 1853 was 248 (compiled from the Maury log-book extracts in the National Archives). This is double the number in any other year. See also Cutler, *op. cit.,* 261.

[25] The following account is taken from the Percy Chase Manuscripts, *Sovereign of the Seas;* this narrative is by a seaman named Faulkner—no first name is indicated.

McKay was presented with an inscribed service of plate by the insurance underwriters to express their appreciation for his skill and ability in refitting his dismasted ship at sea.

From the Cape we had head winds, calms and gales by turns. . . . On the night of October 12th, during a heavy gale, but carrying, as usual, a press of canvas, the maintopmast trestletrees settled, which slackened the topmast backstays, and away went the topmast over the side, taking with it the fore topmast, foreyard and mizzen-top-gallant mast, and every stitch of canvas on the foremast. . . . The hands were called, the ship hove too; and "now" said he to the second mate, (acting mate,) [first mate had been relieved for insubordination] "you take the mainmast, and I will take the foremast, and let us clear the wreck. Remember everything must be saved nothing must be cut. . . ."

Before sunset the next day everything was on board and the ship under her mainsail crossjack course and mizzen-topsail, was balling off 12 knots. . . . In a week both topmasts, topsail yards and foreyard were aloft and the sails bent, and in 12 days the ship was once more taut. . . .

We arrived here [San Francisco] . . . having beaten every vessel that sailed within a month of us. We spoke and passed several vessels on the passage, and went by them as if they had been at anchor. The ship has frequently balled off 18 knots; but never had a steady breeze to test her full speed, yet she made one day, running dead before the wind, 372 miles.

She crossed to Honolulu, took on 8,000 barrels of whale oil, and made the return voyage round the Horn to New York in 80 days. En route, she averaged better than 300 miles per day for 10 consecutive days, a record not surpassed by steamers until years after the Civil War. Hers are perhaps the most remarkable of all Cape Horn clipper passages to California and return.

The greatest year of the clippers was 1853. More passages were made, their average elapsed time lower, and their cargoes heavier than in any other. Virtually every "shipbuilder in the United States launched his clipper *beau ideal*."[26] Never before or after was there such an abundance of glamor in the United States merchant marine. On several occasions three clippers stood in through the Golden Gate within 24 hours, and on two others, five arrived within 48 hours.[27] Notwithstanding unusually heavy weather in the Cape Horn region, a number of new records were set. Less than a month after McKay's great voyage home, the *Northern Light,* driven all the way by her master, Freeman Hatch, completed the passage from San Francisco to New York in 76 days. Hatch was so impressed with the accomplishment that he asked that it be recorded on his tombstone with no other data except his name. And it was.[28]

---

[26] *U.S.J.,* II (April–September, 1855), 213.

[27] San Francisco *Evening Bulletin,* December 16, 1856, p. 1, describes the race between the *Wild Pigeon, John Gilpin, Flying Fish,* and *Trade Wind.* Maury, *op. cit.,* 654 ff., discusses the record passages.

[28] Cutler, *op. cit.,* 268.

It became increasingly clear, as the year drew to a close, that the clipper era was fading. There was not enough business on the Pacific coast to employ more than a fraction of the new clippers—not to mention the old ones, many of which were lying at Boston or New York docks, unable to secure a charter.[29] The California market was no longer of bonanza proportions, and British shipowners were building their own clippers or buying American vessels to recover the China tea trade. Early in the year, some of the finest ships entered the Peruvian guano trade; as the year wore on, many clipper owners were forced to choose between entering this trade or laying up their vessels indefinitely. Those without scruples, could still find useful employment for clippers in the wretched Chinese coolie business or the African slave trade, but even these opportunities were limited.[30] In any case, speed no longer commanded a premium, and the California clippers experienced a period of depression that—though temporary—was a warning of what was to come with finality in 1857.

The fetish for speed continued, but it was a false position, for fast vessels were not necessary to reach normal markets. The sharp clippers had made a profound impression upon maritime commerce, nevertheless, and as business improved, shipowners contracted for the building of vessels which were clippers from the waterline up but which possessed considerably fuller lines below. These "medium" clippers were virtually as fast as the older types and in addition could carry almost twice the amount of freight in proportion to their tonnage. As more ships of this type were built, they claimed their share of record passages, including the record pilot to pilot run of 89 days, 4 hours, from New York to San Francisco, made by the *Andrew Jackson* in 1860,[31] under Captain Jack Williams.

The number of clearances of San Francisco-bound clippers from Atlantic ports dropped to 111 in 1854, and the trend continued downward in 1855. Neither of these years included record-breaking runs, but the latter year marked the opening of the Panama Railroad, which was to deprive the clippers of their best freight accounts, thereby contributing further to the decline of their importance.[32] Significantly, clipper traffic round the Horn decreased proportionately with the fall of New York–

[29] Albion, *op. cit.*, 362; Morison, *op. cit.*, 340.

[30] Percy Chase Manuscripts, Ship *Montauk,* describes the clandestine slaving operations of this vessel off the African coast. The slaves were sold in Havana.

[31] Her log is reprinted in Cutler, *op. cit.*, Appendix VI.

[32] John Haskell Kemble, *The Panama Route, 1848–1869* (Berkeley, 1943), 194.

San Francisco freight rates. The $60.00 per ton rates of 1850 had fallen to $30.00 by 1853, $13.00 in 1855, $10.00 in 1857, and $7.50 in 1858.[33]

Hard passages, small freight loadings, and more and more available vessels characterized 1856. The larger fleet was a result of the conclusion of the Crimean War. American ships chartered by the British and French governments were now released to their American owners, who made every effort to return them to the lanes of normal commerce. Those vessels able to secure enough cargo for a San Francisco voyage encountered considerable difficulty off Cape Horn, where the strongest gales of the decade were blowing. The *Competitor* took eighty days to work round. The *Rapid* was so roughly handled that she was all but dismasted, had most of her canvas torn to shreds, and was forced to put back to Rio de Janeiro with five-sixths of her crew dead or seriously injured.[34] On the way back, Captain Winsor passed the *Neptune's Car*, which, to his extreme annoyance, ignored his distress signal. She had good reason. Her captain, Jacob Patten, had been struck down by brain fever and was lying helpless in his cabin. The first officer was under arrest for insubordination, and the second officer was incompetent to assume command. At this juncture, Mrs. Patten, a nineteen-year-old girl, took command of the vessel, fought the ship westward round the cape, and finally brought her in through the Golden Gate ten days ahead of another crack clipper that had cleared New York with her.[35] Parenthetically, her performance was used by the newly organized woman's rights movement as proof of woman's ability to compete successfully in the pursuits and avocations of man.

Fewer than 100 clippers cleared New York for San Francisco during the year, and only 68 made the voyage in 1857.[36] The *Great Republic*, the largest clipper ever built, and carrying the greatest cargo yet brought round the Horn under sail, made the only noteworthy passage of the year. Commanded by Joseph Limeburner, she dropped anchor off San Francisco 92 days out of New York, having taken only 9 days to traverse the vexing thousand miles of ocean between 50 degrees south in the Atlantic and 50 degrees south in the Pacific.[37] She was almost lost off the Horn on her return voyage; a giant wave crashed upon her deck and

[33] Annual *Report* of the Chamber of Commerce of the State of New York, 1858, p. 235.

[34] See the account in Felix Riesenberg, *Cape Horn* (New York, 1939), 306–307.

[35] *U.S.J.*, V (October, 1856–March, 1857), 458, describes the circumstances and the voyage.

[36] Cutler, *op. cit.*, 331.

[37] See the accounts in *The Friend* (Honolulu), XV (1858) 67; and Francis B. Bradlee, "The Ship *Great Republic* and Donald McKay, Her Builder," Essex Institute *Collections*, LXIII (1927), 193–216, 309–322.

filled her with so much water that she was forced to put in to the Falkland Islands in distress.

With the autumn of 1857 came the panic and depression of that year and, along with it, the end of the enthusiasm that had helped to create and sustain the clippers. To be sure, there was renewed interest subsequently, but the best business had been lost to the Panama route, and commercial capital was no longer ready to invest in ocean sail transportation. Moreover, the sharp clippers had been driven to death.[38] The older vessels—and most of them were four years old or more—were no longer sufficiently sound to attempt ocean passages under full sail. Consequently, the business slump was a mortal blow to the clipper era. The few vessels that remained in service at the outbreak of the Civil War were captured and destroyed by the Confederate cruisers, or sold abroad to avoid destruction. Some remained in, or were built for, the guano and grain trades, but the era of lofty racing queens and premium cargoes had passed.

From the standpoint of shippers, shipowners, and jobbers, the clippers performed well. Most shipments reached their destination intact and soon enough to be advantageous to the consignees. At first a number of cargoes were damaged by moisture, because the heated air between decks tended to rise in the cool Cape Horn latitudes, then condense on the lower side of the decks and run back upon the boxed freight.[39] This was particularly annoying to San Francisco merchants, who were compelled to pay their freight bills before their goods were released; but proper ventilation of the ships' holds soon remedied this fault. The low rates of freight insurance—2 to 3 per cent—which prevailed during the 'fifties reflect the excellence and security of clipper transportation.[40]

Clipper masters were well paid for their professional services and not infrequently owned an interest in their vessel.[41] But men before the mast did not share in the prosperity. Their rate of pay, the conditions under which most of them worked, and the manner in which their services were

---

[38] *U.S.J.*, IV (March, 1856–October, 1856), 4, and VI (April, 1857–September, 1857), 349 ff., show the deterioration of the clippers resulting from the hard driving which they had undergone; the effect of adverse business conditions on shipping is also made clear.

[39] *U.S.J.*, II (October, 1854–September, 1855), 451, describes the problem and its solution.

[40] See the entries for 1850–1860 in the Risk Book of the Mercantile Marine Insurance Company of Boston, in the Baker Library, Harvard University. This company—now the American Central Fire Insurance Company—wrote a large proportion of the policies in the Boston and New York to California run.

[41] See the following memoirs: John D. Whidden, *Ocean Life in the Old Sailing Ship Days* (Boston, 1908); Samuel Samuels, *From the Forecastle to the Cabin* (New York, 1887); William D. Phelps [Webfoot, pseud.], *Fore and Aft; or, Leaves from the Life of an Old Sailor* (Boston, 1871); Clark, *op. cit.*, all *passim*.

secured were deplorable. That most of them were not American citizens explains the general lack of public interest in their behalf; but it is difficult to reconcile $10.00 per month, the average wage on a California clipper, with freight rates of $60.00 per ton.[42] Their lot was not appreciably improved until the passage of La Follette's Seaman's Act two generations later.[43]

Passengers fared somewhat better.[44] But they were carried incidentally and in small numbers compared to the swarm of emigrants and travelers who went to California by way of the overland and Panama routes. Clippers were designed to carry premium freight at maximum speed; there was little concern for passengers in an overloaded, oversparred ship.

The passing of the towering clippers from public attention in the late 'fifties foreshadowed the passing of the United States as a leading commercial and maritime nation of the nineteenth century. The blazing records of the *Flying Cloud, Great Republic, et al.,* were in part the result of unusual economic conditions; when the situation reverted to normal, the interests of the American people were drawn to other matters far removed from maritime enterprise: the Civil War, Reconstruction, the exploitation of the West, the industrialization of the nation. These responsibilities and opportunities left little room in the national house for ocean commerce.

Yet the California clippers had had a fair share in facilitating the westward expansion of the United States, and, for a moment, they had made the American merchant marine the greatest in the world. No nobler or more ephemeral ships would ever pass Cape Horn.

[42] *U.S.J.,* V (October, 1856–March, 1857), 303; Morison, *op. cit.,* 353.

[43] The record kept by virtually every seaman tells the same story of niggardliness and brutality; see Sargent S. Day, Log Book of Seven Voyages, on board Ships *Austerlitz, Shooting Star,* and *Washington Allston,* 1851–1854, MS in the New York Public Library; and Harpur A. Gosnell, *Before the Mast in the Clippers* (New York, 1937).

[44] Two full accounts by passengers are Lyman H. Ellingwood, Journal Kept on board Ship *Dashing Wave,* Voyages from Boston to San Francisco, Thence to Shanghai, Hong Kong, Singapore, Calcutta, Boston, MS on deposit in the Essex Institute, Salem; and Helper, *op. cit.,* aboard the *Staghound.*

Pioneer Protestant Preachers of Early California

ROCKWELL D. HUNT

[For many years professor of history and dean of the graduate school in the University of Southern California, Rockwell D. Hunt is now director of the California History Foundation at his alma mater, the College of the Pacific. His writings include *John Bidwell, Prince of California Pioneers* (Caldwell, Idaho, 1942) and *California Ghost Towns Live Again* (Stockton, 1948).]

UNQUESTIONABLY life in California's gold days was characterized by highly pathological conditions, even to the extent of social insanities. Most of the gold hunters were young men, homeless, far away from the counsel and restraints of the family fireside. The nature of their feverish daily occupation made it strikingly akin to gambling—the whirl and the excitement of it all made outright gambling seem a natural if not inevitable concomitant. To the casual onlooker gambling could easily have appeared to be universal. The same might be said of drinking. And, it may be added, both practices are quite understandable. The moral atmosphere was rather despairingly appraised by William Roberts, Superintendent of the Oregon and California Methodist Mission Conference, who wrote in a letter from Oregon City to Isaac Owen, September 26, 1849, "Oh tell me about that land of wickedness and gold and death: is there any salvation?"

It has long been a favorite indoor sport of authors, script writers, and not a few popular lecturers to aver, or at least broadly to insinuate, that in the hectic days of '49 *everybody* was doing it. "Judges and clergymen used to elbow their way, so one remembered, to the tables, and used to play with the rest." That the few women of the community were generally degenerate "fancy ladies" is taken for granted—there is virtually no historical record of respectable women of the period. Did all of those thousands of adventurers who trekked to California park their morals east of the Missouri? And did the hordes of Argonauts who rounded the Horn or crossed the isthmus sink their ethical ideals in the depths of the Pacific?

Such distortions of the real truth, reiterated with grotesque exaggeration in the "tall yarns" of the old-timer and pseudo historian, have been eagerly seized upon by the sensationmonger and frequently by misguided persons who, fleeing from their own moral obligations, have sought refuge behind a flimsy defense mechanism. Josiah Royce tells of a frequently repeated pioneer absurdity about the "one lady in San Francisco, and she a newcomer, who was reverently, silently, and sentimentally worshiped by the vast, rude and drunken throngs about her." Another scandalous assertion was to the effect that in early San Francisco there were no "ladies" at all.

It is of record that through worthy, accredited representatives, the Christian church, long recognized as one of the three great conservative forces of human society (with family and school), quickly made its appearance in delirious San Francisco. It is likewise of record that the pioneer preachers who, if irresponsible gossip were gospel truth, promptly lost their religion to turn bartenders and gamblers, were, as Royce, himself the son of a noble pioneer mother, has concluded, "on the whole remarkably faithful, intelligent, laborious, and devout. One would have suffered sadly without them." Even more cogent and convincing is the testimony of the contemporary authors of the invaluable *Annals of San Francisco*: "... the self-sacrificing efforts of the clergymen who immigrated here cannot be too highly estimated." The thoughtless celebrant of the California centennial years would be well advised to note carefully the summation by the industrious annalists, published in 1855:

We have said enough, we hope, to prove that not all, nor nigh all the citizens of San Francisco are lost to everything but reckless dissipation. No city of equal size—few of ten times its age—can present such a list of men and institutions, who have accomplished so much *real* good, with so little of cant and hypocrisy.[1]

A recent tour of the twenty-one Franciscan mission sites of Alta California, from San Diego in the south to Sonoma in the north, has brought to the present writer fresh appreciation of the stupendous labors and deep devotion of the disciples of St. Francis of Assisi in their efforts to convert and civilize the rude aborigines. The story of these Catholic missions has been told and retold. They constitute the subject of a very ample literature; the restoration of their buildings has become an object of pride to loyal Californians. They have deservedly become an esteemed part of our rich heritage. Still, it can never be forgotten that, cruelly secularized and destroyed in the years of the Mexican régime, they can never be restored to the status of original, active institutions. It is now almost as if they had never been—they live chiefly in memory.

If the religious influence during pre-American periods was almost wholly Catholic, it is equally true that Protestants of various denomina-

[1] Frank Soulé, John H. Gihon, and James Nisbet, *The Annals of San Francisco* (New York, 1855), 701.

tions had a prominent part in placing foundation stones for the super-structure of the great American commonwealth of California. Indeed, this factor is in evidence as early as the appearance in 1826 of Jedediah Strong Smith, sometimes called the "Bible toter," the first American to come overland to California. This devout young Christian trapper is belatedly receiving recognition for his personal character and the far-reaching influence of his expedition.

But our present concern is with the pioneer missionaries and preachers of the Protestant faith in the early American period of California history, not in the least disparaging, however, the influence of individual laymen or such bands of Argonauts as the "Boston and California Mining Company," whose members were exhorted by Harvard's President Edward Everett to go to California "with the Bible in one hand and your New England civilization in the other and make your mark on the people and country."

In view of the abnormal situation then obtaining in San Francisco and the mining centers, there is no gainsaying the great need for missionary work! In June, 1853, the *California Christian Advocate* "found, *by actual count,* the whole number of places where liquor is sold in this city [San Francisco] to be 537.... There were 556 bar tenders in the various places at the time when the memoranda were taken. We think we may safely add one-quarter, if not one-third, as reserve corps, making, including women, 743 bar tenders in our city." Gambling houses and dance halls of low repute were fully in proportion.

Truth requires that we add, however, there was a brighter side. In the *Annals* we read: "Happily, the long record of vice and immorality (the black pages of our diary) has a bright and noble counterpart, like the gold-dust among the muddy atoms of our own river-beds, that redeems our character from wholesale condemnation."[2]

This phase is well illustrated by a graphic picture of the inspiring audiences Reverend Albert Williams, a pioneer Presbyterian minister, paints for us: "These were mostly in the prime of manhood. There were few, very few gray hairs then seen. Such an assemblage of educated, active, strong men, rarely brought together in any land, it was a pleasure to look upon, as it was my own privilege weekly ..."[3]

Enough has been said to make it clear that early California society was by no means overlooked by various Protestant church and missionary

---

[2] *Ibid.,* 687.

[3] Albert Williams, *A Pioneer Pastorate and Times* (San Francisco, 1879), 141.

organizations. If saloons and gambling halls were symptoms of wide-spread dissoluteness, the churches stood faithfully by as health-giving agencies. Therefore, in the interest of historical veracity and true perspective, and as a corrective to the too-flippant assumption of the absence of moral fiber and religious conviction, due recognition for the important role enacted by staunch Christian leaders must be given. Their marching orders came as if issued from the slopes of Olivet—and faithfully were they heeded. Soon after the discovery of gold became known in the East the first commissioned missionaries of the American Home Missionary Society received these far-reaching instructions:

We wish you to take a broad and comprehensive survey of the work to be done there. Never were men more emphatically called to lay foundations—foundations that are not to have ages to consolidate them before they are built on, but which are to have a massive, and, we trust, a beautiful and enduring superstructure erected upon them at once.[4]

The pioneer preacher was far more than a preacher. The functions that he performed, the tasks that fell into his hands demanded more of him than the vocation of clergyman. It was incumbent upon him to become a public servant, with humane instincts, benevolent heart, ready to respond to any call for help from people of every station in life.

Numerous Protestant denominations were ably represented. Almost from the beginning of the gold excitement there were Congregationalists, Presbyterians, Methodists, Baptists, and Episcopalians, who may be labeled forty-niners, and still others appeared shortly afterward. It would be inaccurate to state that there was no rivalry among denominational leaders. The catholicity of spirit, however, and the practice of tolerance were strongly in evidence. The helping hand was generously extended; the church facilities of one denomination were placed at the disposal of a newcomer of another communion, and the true sentiment of Christian brotherhood was exemplified in a remarkable degree. A single striking illustration is seen in the dedication services, in 1853, of the First Unitarian Church, organized in 1850. Participating were Martin C. Briggs of the Methodist Episcopal Church, J. W. Brierly of the Baptist Church, and Jesse Boring of the Methodist Church South.

No attempt can be made in this paper to set forth the deeds of all the pioneer Protestant preachers of California, nor to present a complete list of their names. To arrive at a reasonable view of the subject, however, and to reach a just appraisal of factors involved, it is important to

---

[4] Quoted by W. W. Ferrier, "Origin and Growth of the Protestant Church," in *Religious Progress on the Pacific Slope* (Boston, 1917), 65.

deal briefly with certain leaders whose careers show generic quality, whose lives illuminate the subject in hand.

Samuel Hopkins Willey, a young graduate of Dartmouth, reached Monterey in February, 1849, just as the gold fever was mounting to its dizzy height, bearing a commission from the Home Missionary Society of the Congregational Church. In the autumn of that year he was made a chaplain of the historic Constitutional Convention, meeting in Colton Hall, Monterey. Willey served also as chaplain at the Presidio, and for six months he conducted a pioneer school in Monterey. For many years he carried on the regular work of Howard Presbyterian Church in San Francisco, of which he was chief founder.

But Samuel Willey is best known and gratefully remembered for his fruitful endeavors in the field of education. He had been planning for a college or university even before the end of 1849. Adverse conditions brought delay but not defeat. Encouraged by him, Henry Durant opened a preparatory school in Oakland, in 1853. Two years later the charter of the College of California, a Christian institution, was granted. It was dedicated in 1860, and later became the University of California. While never president, Willey served as actual head administrator of the College of California for some eight years. At the Golden Jubilee of the university, on April 16, 1910, President Benjamin Ide Wheeler conferred upon venerable Samuel Willey, in the presence of ten thousand persons, an honorary degree, citing him as "founder, prophet, seer, beholder," and announcing, "Upon you, the foremost benefactor of California, first citizen of the state, I confer the degree of Doctor of Laws."

Not least among Willey's many contributions are the products of his pen. His *History of the College of California* was published in 1887. Of special value as historical documents are his *Thirty Years in California* (1849–1879) and *The Transition Period of California* (1846–1850).

"To the Reverend Timothy Dwight Hunt, D.D., belongs the honor of being the first Presbyterian minister to engage in Christian work in California."[5] He had arrived in San Francisco on October 29, 1848, thus antedating most Protestant missionaries in California.

It is proper to explain that Hunt came not from New York, where he was a member of the Genesee Presbytery, but from Honolulu, having gone in 1844 to the Sandwich Islands as a missionary of the American Board of Commissioners of Foreign Missions. Later he entered upon work for the Americans resident there.

---

[5] Edward Arthur Wicher. *The Presbyterian Church in California, 1849–1927* (New York, 1927), 38.

When the exciting news of gold discovery reached the Islands, his congregation was quickly dissolved; members vanished like the dew of the morning. There was no stopping the exodus to the land of gold. His next move was to obtain a leave of absence for a period of three months, "with the privilege of continued absence or return, as Providence should indicate."

In San Francisco at the time of Hunt's arrival there were a few scattered members of different Protestant denominations, scarcely sufficient to justify the organization of a church. It seemed wise to undertake some form of united Christian endeavor, without special emphasis on any denomination. Very shortly after landing, therefore, Hunt was made chaplain at large to the town of San Francisco for one year, at a salary of $2,500. He maintained a union religious service and performed other religious functions.

Scenes in San Francisco shifted daily in kaleidoscopic manner. Hunt was a Presbyterian of the New School and is credited with being the founder of the first Presbyterian church in California; but that did not prevent his becoming the first pastor of the First Congregational Church, of which the services for a time were conducted in the little schoolhouse on Portsmouth Square.

Like his fellow worker Samuel H. Willey, Hunt, who had been educated at Yale College, was deeply interested in establishing a non-denominational college in California. He was one of the first men to be chosen for the board of trustees of the school known as the College of California.

"Reminiscences of Early Life in California" is the general title of a series of twelve articles by Hunt published in *The Pacific* in 1888 and 1889. W. W. Ferrier considered his article "The Arrival of the First Steamer," as supplemented by "The Arrival of the First Missionaries," as "probably the most graphic and interesting account of that historic event extant."[6]

On the first of February, 1849, Albert Williams of Clinton, New Jersey, made this entry in his diary:

"After a pastorate in this place of ten years, I this day received a joint commission from the Boards of Education and Missions of the Presbyterian Church, to proceed forthwith to the new field of Christian, as it is also of secular enterprise, in Upper California."[7]

---

[6] W. W. Ferrier, *Ninety Years of Education in California, 1846–1936* (Berkeley, 1937), 385.
[7] Williams, *op. cit.,* 1.

He was soon on his way to the new-found land of El Dorado. After an enforced delay on the Isthmus of Panama, the famous ship *Oregon* carried him to port in San Francisco, where he landed on April 1. The First Presbyterian Church of San Francisco was formally organized on May 20, an occasion of mutual congratulations to participants. Williams, the new leader, enjoyed cordial and helpful relationship with no less authorities than General Persifor Smith and Commodore Thomas ap Catesby Jones.

After a trying period during which church services were held in the public schoolhouse, then in a tent, a new building sent out from New York via Cape Horn arrived in the autumn of 1850, only to be destroyed by a terrific windstorm. Other misfortunes followed—the disastrous fires of the city took their heavy toll.

The reconstructed church was dedicated in January, 1851, with thirty-two ladies present, the largest number of women in any San Francisco congregation to that date. A few days later the sixth great fire completely destroyed the building.

The comparatively brief ministry of Albert Williams was filled with intense activity, unremitting toil, and complete devotion. Among his extrapastoral functions was the founding of such organizations as the Bible Society of San Francisco, the Seamen's Friend Society, and the Benevolent Society.

In his *A Pioneer Pastorate and Times* Williams has given us a faithful picture of religious and social conditions among "an unsettled and migratory people." He was a man of great versatility, receiving out-of-town calls with increasing frequency. In a day when moral evils "cast their gloomy shade over the social masses," he won and held the solid respect of the community in which he labored.

Two Methodist pioneers must be introduced together—Isaac Owen and William Taylor. Pursuant to an action taken by the General Conference of the Methodist Episcopal Church in 1848, Bishop Beverly Waugh was charged with the responsibility of selecting two missionaries for the California field. The Bishop's first selection was Isaac Owen, a native of Vermont, whose first education was received in a log schoolhouse. After expressing full confidence in his judgment, prudence, integrity, piety, and zeal, the Bishop's letter continues: "You will be the honored instrument in laying the foundation of the Methodist system of preaching the Gospel in that distant field where, by grace, its achievements will be glorious in bringing many sons of God to glory."

The other appointee was William Taylor. The oldest of a family of five sons and six daughters, William had been brought up as a farmer lad and had begun preaching at twenty-one. Of all the pioneer religious personalities of the Golden State he was destined to become the most outstanding.

Owen came to California overland in a covered wagon. As a single indication of the obstacles encountered en route it is sufficient to note that the fifteen oxen with which the party started were gradually reduced to six. Owen's first California sermon was preached in the shade of an oak tree in Grass Valley, in September, 1849.

Taylor came round the Horn on the Baltimore clipper *Andalusia,* arriving safely within the Golden Gate on September 21, after a tedious voyage of 155 days. Learning of his appointment to the San Francisco station by Superintendent William Roberts of the Oregon and California Missionary Conference, he set to work with a will. Owen's appointment was to Sacramento.

The conditions that confronted William Taylor in the autumn of 1849 can today be scarcely imagined. Prices were fantastically high, the housing problem was incredibly difficult, there was virtually no stable population, the masses of inrushing Argonauts in their mad search for gold seemed bereft of morals and social responsibility. But William Taylor was not one to take defeat for an answer. In short order he won wide reputation as a street preacher. Perched on a goods box or whisky barrel, he had no difficulty in "singing up" a crowd of men; then he preached, often to crowds numbering several thousands, for his baritone voice was powerful and resonant. He came to be known as "California Taylor."

Seven years of strenuous but fruitful labor he devoted to California. Three of his books afforded clear insight into his life and activities: *Seven Years of Street Preaching, California Life Illustrated,* and *An Autobiography.* Of the gracious and beneficent influence of his ministry there can be no doubt. David Starr Jordan pronounced him "the most prominent evangelical reformer of his day, a great force for good in San Francisco." Yet his work in California was but a prelude to a distinguished career in Canada, Europe, Egypt and Palestine, Australia, and elsewhere, particularly as Missionary Bishop of Africa. His sunset days were spent in his loved California, where death took him in 1902.

Meanwhile, Isaac Owen, whose long service as Presiding Elder brought him the title "Elder Owen," became noted for his conscientiousness, and was regarded with affection for his brotherly spirit and the purity of his motives. He was respected for his ability and perseverance in every undertaking.

Two of his major contributions must be mentioned. More than any other person, Owen is credited with being the founder of the College of the Pacific, first called California Wesleyan College, the original charter of which was dated July 10, 1851. Referring to his zeal for education, ". . . it has been said hyperbolically that if he could have had his way he would have had 'a high school at every crossroad and a college in every county.' "[8]

The other noteworthy contribution was the result of his foresight as founder of the Methodist Book Concern in San Francisco. Before leaving New York he had received aid which enabled him to ship around the Horn books to the value of some $2,000. These became the foundation of the California establishment. William Taylor in his autobiography, tells of the actual beginnings:

February 10, 1850, Brother Owen and I, assisted by a few brethern, dug the foundation and commenced the erection of a small Book Room adjoining our church on Powell Street. Carpenters' wages were $12 a day, so, being unable to pay such prices, we did the work with our own hands, and did not consider it a hardship.[9]

In his zeal for books Owen was religiously heeding the injunction of John Wesley, who had urged this service. "Carry books with you on every round," he said, "leave no stone unturned in this work."[10]

Another "mighty man of Methodism" arrived at San Francisco on September 17, 1850. This was Martin C. Briggs, a native of Oneida County, New York. Immediately he became a tower of strength to the moral and religious forces of California. He was largely instrumental in establishing the Annual Conference and in launching *The California Christian Advocate,* of which he became co-editor with S. D. Simonds. He had a prominent part in founding the University of the Pacific, of which he later became president, and which he served for many years as a trustee.

As editor and as preacher Briggs had definite convictions, and these he expressed with directness and force, without equivocation. His was not the "art of fence-rider." His style and manner compelled attention; he was a rugged moralist, not devoid of a subtle sense of humor, a terror to the evildoer.

---

[8] Ferrier, *op. cit.,* 189.

[9] *William Taylor of California: An Autobiography* (revised ed., London, 1897), 534.

[10] Abel Stevens, *A Compendious History of American Methodism* (New York, 1867), 534.

In the dark days of civil strife, he rendered invaluable service toward preserving California to the Union. He boldly exposed plans for division of the state; he spoke out fearlessly from pulpit and platform, as a patriotic, militant orator, winning a place alongside Thomas Starr King, Leland Stanford, and John Bidwell, great champions of freedom.

In Briggs we find the stuff of which real leaders of men are made. All in all, he must be regarded as the most conspicuous of the honorable body of California Pioneer Methodists whose activities continued through many years. The qualities of the man were admirably summarized in a tribute by Elbert R. Dille, who referred to him as the "Modern Nestor of the Conference," and said, in part:

Doctor Briggs had qualities of mind and heart that gave him stature above other men. . . . If Doctor Briggs was a terror to evil-doers, if his speech was lightning, if he could be as a thunder-bolt smiting evil, only those who were rebuked by his denunciations of wrong were ever repelled by him. Those who loved righteousness and prayed for the redemption of our nation from its sin and shame, knew the gentleness as well as the strength of the man.[11]

Doctor A. C. Hirst concluded his appraisal by declaring "His commanding personality has been a leading factor in shaping the Methodism of California.[12]

To Osgood C. Wheeler goes the distinction of being the founder of the first Baptist church in San Francisco (July 6, 1849). He had arrived on the last day of February of that year on the *California,* the first steamship to enter the Golden Gate.

Before entering upon his important missionary labors, in his thirty-ninth year, Wheeler had equipped himself well with education and actual experience. The invitation to proceed to California came from the American Baptist Home Missionary Society. In the fourteen days he had to make all arrangements, "he resigned his pastorate, closed up all his business affairs, visited Philadelphia, preached ten times, gave three addresses, and superintended the getting together of his outfit."

Intense activities began at once when Wheeler stepped ashore in San Francisco. He became an organizer and the first moderator of the Baptist Association; he helped organize the California Baptist Education Society, of which he was first president; he was editor of the first Baptist newspaper west of the Rocky Mountains, published in Sacramento. Likewise he was president of the Pacific Tract Society, a leader in the temperance

---

[11] *California Christian Advocate,* September 16, 1926.

[12] A. C. Hirst, "Methodism in California," *The Californian Illustrated Magazine,* III (December, 1892), 107.

movement, and a public speaker whose splendid ability brought frequent requests from varied parts of the state.

In the midst of his labors, in the summer of 1850, a throat infection necessitated his retirement from the active ministry—for seven years he was unable to speak in public. Even so, he served with fidelity and efficiency in other capacities. Years later he partially recovered from his throat trouble and resumed his preaching and speaking throughout California. In 1889 Wheeler presented a paper before the California Baptist Historical Society, in Sacramento, describing in detail the memorable scene of October 21, 1849, at North Beach, San Francisco, when the ordinance of baptism was administered.[13] The other churches had suspended their morning service. "Their pastors, with their officers, and the body of their congregations, were present and joined in the procession." Attending also were the mayor, Commodore Jones, the prime minister of the Hawaiian Kingdom, and numerous other officials.

Following his death, on April 16, 1891, the Oakland *Evening Tribune* paid him this tribute: "Captain Wheeler was a man universally liked, and his friends all over the state are legion. He has had a long and eventful career, and his early advent to the Golden State has made his life a part of the early history of California." Such personal traits as he possessed in generous measure are an invaluable asset to any community—"a burning energy, indomitable perseverance and courage, good cheer, rare tact, blended with inborn courtesy."

Joseph A. Benton was another great religious leader. As an illustration of the speed of events in the gold days, it may be noted that Benton arrived in San Francisco on July 6, 1849; on the twenty-second of the same month he preached his first sermon in Sacramento; and on September 23 the first Congregational church of that city was organized.

Was he but a brilliant dreamer when in 1850 he delivered a Thanksgiving sermon on "California as She Was, as She Is, and as She Is to Be"? He boldly declared, "The world's center will change; this will be the land of pilgrimage, and no man will be thought to have seen the world till he has seen California."[14]

Benton had come round the Horn on the *Edward Everett* as chaplain of a mining and trading company. After the company disbanded he entered upon "a work for religion and education in California which has come

[13] Frank Dixon, "Baptists in California," *Californian Illustrated Magazine,* II (August, 1892), 442 ff.
[14] Quoted in *Religious Progress in the Pacific Slope,* 70.

down the years with imperishable influence."[15] On one occasion he was introduced by Horace Bushnell as "the father and mother of Congregationalism in California."

He met with S. H. Willey and S. V. Blakeslee in Sacramento on October 22, 1849, in what Dr. Ferrier calls "the first organized movement for an institution of higher learning in California."[16] It was several years before the College of California was actually founded.

In August, 1851, *The Pacific,* a weekly publication of the Congregational Church, came into being. Joseph A. Benton became its distinguished editor, in which capacity his work was comparable to that of Martin C. Briggs of the *California Christian Advocate.* From its first issue this paper was a staunch defender and strong advocate of free education—"schools which shall be as free to all classes of the community as the air we breathe."

Mention must be made of J. L. Ver Mehr, one of the two first Episcopalian rectors in California. He and F. S. Mines reached San Francisco in 1849. Grace Episcopal Church, on Powell Street, began its service in October in a modest way under Ver Mehr; it was formally organized into a parish on April 28, 1850. In the meantime, both rectors had opened parish schools. Indeed, Ver Mehr gave the major part of his time and effort for years to educational work in San Francisco and Sonoma. His own book, written years afterward, is *My Checkered Life.*

Other names deserve a place in any list of the California pioneer preachers, though it would exceed the limits of the present article to attempt details. Sylvester Woodbridge, staunch Presbyterian Covenanter, was commissioned to come to California in 1848 and reached San Francisco early in 1849. Of him it was said that he was "slow in coming to a conclusion, but immovable as a mountain when he believed his position was right."[17] He organized the first Presbyterian church of California in the town of Benicia, where he doggedly remained for eighteen years, despite the vanished dream of Benicia's greatness. Of his many activities one of the most fruitful is seen in the establishment, at a later date, of the religious paper, *The Occident,* in San Francisco.

After a dreadful voyage of nearly eight months, James Woods, a young Presbyterian minister with wife and three small children, entered the Golden Gate early in 1850, completing the "Three W's" who constituted the first presbytery—Woodbridge, Williams, Woods. He served many

---

[15] Ferrier, *op. cit.,* 32.
[16] *Ibid.,* 177.
[17] Wicher, *op. cit.,* 39.

years in numerous churches as a faithful minister, his longest pastorate being in Stockton. He has left a record of his labors in *Recollections of Pioneer Work in California,* published in 1878.

Others there were, every whit as worthy as those presented above— godly men like A. S. Gibbons, O. P. Fitzgerald, W. A. Scott, J. W. Douglas, Frederick Buel, Charles Maclay, Frederick Gray, and still others, of various religious denominations, many of forgotten names. Some reached California at later dates, yet were not disobedient to their vision, meriting the title seer, or prophet.

The main thesis of this paper is twofold: (1) that the pioneer Protestant preachers in California had a significant part, with salutary influence, in the drama of the gold rush and the building of the state; (2) that no true perspective of that stirring, vital period is possible which ignores or minimizes this factor in the whole complex picture.

Most of the pioneer preachers were young men; "many of them were but striplings in the ministry." The reason that those mentioned were active chiefly in San Francisco and northern California is that during the early mining days the incoming hordes flocked to that part of the state. Others, no less devoted, labored in southern California at somewhat later dates.

As a body the early preachers were a noble group of princely pioneers who came to California neither to join the mad scramble for gold nor to exploit their fellow men. Imbued with a spirit of high adventure in the realm of religion, they came with a deep sense of mission as messengers of Christian light, with a profound conviction of the sacredness of their calling. And their coming contributed richly toward redeeming the California gold days from an all-devouring avarice and from sordid living. They did constitute "a bright and noble counterpart, like the gold-dust among the muddy atoms of our own river-beds." Strength of personality, integrity of character, great capacity for endurance, utter willingness to sacrifice for their holy cause, a real passion for godliness— such were the resplendent qualities of their courageous souls and their undaunted spirits.

The Health Factor in the Gold Rush Era

JOHN E. BAUR

[John E. Baur is a graduate student in history in the University of California at Los Angeles.]

IN 1848 a virtually incurable world-wide infection commenced in California. It was the gold fever. The aftereffects of this spiritual malady were often to be homesickness, heartache, wanderlust, and, occasionally, "lead poisoning." But those who contracted this age-old disease carried with them to California far more dangerous physical contagions. They brought illness by land and sea.

Seeking to realize their disappointed dreams of liberty, two shiploads of Germans left Le Havre late in 1848. Both vessels were infected with cholera, and this plague broke out aboard before they reached their respective ports, New York and New Orleans. By January, 1849, the Crescent City was panic stricken, and in a short time river boats carried the disease throughout the Mississippi Valley. St. Louis was attacked, emigrants carried the disease onto the plains, and soon the trail all the way to the continental divide was lined with graves of the victims.

New Orleans was also an important port of embarkation for the isthmian route. At Panama cholera flourished among the Argonauts awaiting Pacific passage, and in October, 1850, San Francisco was affected by this seaward attack.[1] The contagion was even more unmerciful to inland Sacramento. That city's death rate was estimated at 15 per cent, while that of San Jose was 10 per cent. The plague, following isothermal lines, took only 5 per cent of San Franciscans.[2] At its peak, the Sacramento death rate reached twenty a day. With the coming of cooler weather, the epidemic waned, and it ended about December 1. Cholera came again in 1852, but with less force.[3] Its effects upon central California had been great. Death was sudden. As a result, panic occurred in the diggings, where little medicine and medical knowledge existed. Today, it is known that Asiatic cholera is primarily water-borne, making the prevention of epidemics dependent on a good sewage system and an adequate supply of pure water. San Francisco and Sacramento lacked both.

[1] John S. Chambers, *The Conquest of Cholera* (New York, 1938), 242.
[2] Peter H. Burnett, *Recollections and Opinions of an Old Pioneer* (New York, 1880), 376.
[3] John Carr, *Pioneer Days in California* (Eureka, 1891), 86.

The cholera had been a nation-wide evil, only made more acute in California by the scarceness of medical aid. The fever epidemics which struck simultaneously were also, in part, of outside origin, but they were local and lasted longer. As fevers generally were misunderstood, it was difficult to determine with exactness the extent of these ailments and to diagnose them. Malaria was brought from Panama. Although some of those who contracted it thought it native to the gold region, the majority had been stricken at Panama or on shipboard, only to reach California to die. Thus, the early high death rate was an unfair reflection upon the region's climate. Sufferers, too, were quick to blame the Sacramento area for malaria and other fevers, generally classified as brain, typhoid, intermittent, remittent, and continued fevers. To them this was logical, for the current theory was that malaria and several other malarial-type fevers were carried by a specific but mysterious poison generated in the soil. Swamp gases were said to be especially rich in this material, and the upturning of new soil was supposed to release the fatal substances. The tule marshes near Sacramento seemed ideal for the beginning of a plague. In 1850, Dr. James L. Tyson, a well-experienced physician, upholding this view, called these miasmic areas "fit nurseries for disease, which prevails here to an alarming extent during the latter part of summer, and in the fall months, when the water is low."[4] He believed the Sacramento Valley more unhealthful than any part of the Mississippi Valley. With further vilification, the congestive fever prevalent there came to be called "Sacramento Fever." Sometimes this malady lingered for months, but in its more virulent form it affected the brain, often proving fatal. Among the fevers were dysentery, typhoid fever, rheumatic fever, and meningitis, then called brain fever. Here again, sanitation is vital. Typhoid, especially, is water-borne. In the Sacramento mining regions, streams rapidly subsided in summer. Quantities of fish often died in the waters, and the streams, as they reached the valleys, becoming sluggish, purified themselves less rapidly. Crowded mining camps and towns, lacking sanitation, gave impetus to the typhoid and dysentery threat.[5] Sometimes water was boiled, but not frequently enough.

Medical man and miner were concerned over diarrhea—a new, frightful species of "congestive diarrhea." Suffering from the ailment, an Australian doctor despairingly reported that never in his long experience

[4] James L. Tyson, M.D., *Diary of a Physician in California* (New York, 1850), 54–55.
[5] Theodore T. Johnson, *California and Oregon* (Philadelphia, 1851), 178.

had he heard of anything like it. Calling the disease "a combination of fever, ague, and diarrhoea," he described the symptoms—chill and headache followed by burning fever, gas on the stomach, and violent purging.[6] Usually, the illness was fatal. Diarrhea, however, is a symptom rather than a disease. It is characteristic of cholera, dysentery, and typhoid fever. All these diseases were rampant in the California of 1849 to 1855, and, to further preclude an accurate analysis, most types of fevers, cholera, and dysentery, are accompanied by chills, high temperature, thirst, intestinal disorders, and nausea.

Fevers were the result of the lack of proper sanitation and ordinary personal care, but the want of a balanced diet was even swifter in causing dietary-deficiency diseases. Scurvy occurred among those who came by sea, for the early rush was without preparation. Ships were almost always overcrowded. Lime juice was either unprovided or insufficient. Many died at sea, but the majority lingered to succumb in California. It may seem illogical that scurvy was rampant in California itself. Unlike the fevers, its cause was generally known. Numerous, nevertheless, are the descriptions of scurvy sufferers. The answer is simple. California had not as yet begun to produce large crops, and all food was imported at great expense. As a result, the diet of gold seekers usually consisted of salt pork, bacon, flour, beans, and coffee. By 1851, fruits and vegetables could be found in San Francisco's eating places, but, for a time, they were expensive, and they were far from the mining regions. A Methodist missionary, William Taylor, told a group of scurvy sufferers to gather the wild lettuce which grew near San Francisco. After eating this herb, all improved and most fully recovered.[7] Victims, on eating greens, rapidly improved. Deaths, however, were many. Probably, the sufferers, unfamiliar with the wild plants of the new land, feared them almost as much as scurvy.

Dietary shortage took its toll, but some died because they had no diet at all! Starvation in a golden land was a great irony, more so because the miners were noted for their generosity. But this famous charity was emotional and demonstrative rather than reflective and organized. If the cosmopolitan society of diggers had any uniform creed, it was self-help. Those who failed to acquire enough of the yellow substance were likely to starve, and poor hospital care sometimes resulted in starvation even for those who paid high fees.[8]

    [6] J. Hungerford Sealy, M.D., "The State of Medical and Other Affairs in California," *The Lancet,* LIX (1850), 644–645.
    [7] William Taylor, *California Life Illustrated* (New York, 1858), 230–231.
    [8] *Ibid.,* 99.

California flora had mitigated the sufferings of the vitamin-starved, but it could be a curse, too. Then, as now, poison oak abounded in the Sacramento region, and large numbers of gold seekers were exposed to it.[9] Not understanding allergies, California immigrants were puzzled over the immunity of those who could handle the plant while others dared not even stand near it. Various local remedies, discovered on the spot, or offered by native Californians, were tried. The soaproot was used in bathing afflicted skin. This merely allayed the irritation. To effect a cure, a moderate diet was recommended.[10] Others vouched for the results of steam baths. One suggestion, probably seldom followed, was the chewing of poison-oak leaves without swallowing them.[11]

The Bay region, too, offered its maladies, throat and lung afflictions. Almost all visitors praised San Francisco's bracing climate, but warned "weak-chested people" to stay away. Catarrh, pneumonia, bronchitis, consumption, and neuralgia were caused or worsened by the cold winds and dampness. As late as 1880, of the year's city mortality of 5,800, San Francisco lost 505 from pneumonia and 234 from bronchitis and other respiratory disorders.[12] Waxing poetical, an early visitor announced, "You may doctor and bandage your throat as you will, but the sense of its soreness will hang round you still."[13] Nevertheless, some eastern invalids who had heard of the golden sunshine when they heard of the golden hills, came to San Francisco and died there before they could learn of a more agreeable climate.[14]

The winds of the Bay area also contributed to eye diseases. Ophthalmia, inflammation of the eyelid's membrane, was one of California's four distinctive and most prevalent complaints. Almost every afternoon a veritable dust storm swept the unpaved city, causing many coughs and sore eyes. Other optical diseases were common in central California. The glare of the sun and the dryness of the Sacramento Valley atmosphere caused there much eye trouble. Among the diggers, eye disorders resulted also from the evaporation of mercury in open pans.[15]

These were the major illnesses of California from 1849 to 1860, but there were many minor afflictions. Rheumatism was common in the min-

[9] Titus Fay Cronise, *The Natural Wealth of California* (San Francisco, 1868), 351.

[10] William Kelly, *An Excursion to California over the Prairie, Rocky Mountains, and Great Sierra Nevada* (2 vols., London, 1851), II, 27–28.

[11] Isabelle Saxon, *Five Years within the Golden Gate* (London, 1868), 106.

[12] Hubert Howe Bancroft, *History of California* (7 vols.; San Francisco, 1884–1890), VII, 705.

[13] J. A. Boddam-Whetham, *Western Wanderings* (London, 1874), 147.

[14] William I. Kip, *The Early Days of My Episcopate* (New York, 1892), 86.

[15] John S. Hittell, *The Resources of California* (San Francisco, 1868), 367.

ing regions where the washers stood long hours up to their waists in cold, fast-running mountain streams. Smallpox epidemics did not come until the 1860's, when the state was better prepared to fight them. Diphtheria struck in late 1860. In Sacramento, it carried off a large number of children. Social diseases were present, too, but as yet not the great menace that cholera and the fevers had become. Accidents, usually, were individual. There were few mass catastrophes except steamer and steamboat disasters such as the sinking of the *Sagamore* in October, 1851.[16] In San Francisco, fires were frequent, but the public, used to such emergencies, found their losses more material than human. In the mining regions, accidents were common. Avalanches buried or wounded numerous diggers. Falls were not rare, and, of course, there were always knife and bullet wounds, thus putting surgery in the emergency stage.[17] Snakebites and insect bites and stings often occurred.[18]

Alcoholism and its conclusion, delirium tremens, became a common form of mental unbalance. At Stockton, the state insane asylum, established in 1853, never lacked patients.

The Argonauts had heard that California was a climatic paradise. They had learned to envision a sunny land of gentle people, perhaps indolent and pleasure-loving in their pastoral life, but certainly healthy. Now, these immigrants found central California a pesthole. Some blamed the country, others blamed the times; they should all have blamed themselves, for the pioneer community had been made ripe for ill health through the things its inhabitants did, and more, by what they did not do.

A newcomer, as soon as he set foot on California soil, saw the filth of San Francisco. As late as 1854, one of these new arrivals reported that: "The streets were thickly covered with black rotten mud. These were ... made a general depot for all kinds of rubbish and household sweepings, offals and filth."[19] The dead were still contagion spreaders. At Miller's Point, the beach was used as a burial ground, bodies being either covered at high tide with a layer of sand, or carried away by the sea. As a result, the shore became a field of skulls. On another part of the beach was "Happy Valley," more appropriately called "Sickly Valley." In 1850, this was a large gathering of tents, "where filth of every description, and

---

[16] Edouard Auger, *Voyage en Californie* (Paris, 1854), 228–232.

[17] For an excellent discussion of the subject, see George D. Lyman, M.D., "The Scalpel under Three Flags in California," California Historical Society *Quarterly*, IV (1925), 142–206.

[18] William Shaw, *Golden Dreams and Waking Realities* (London, 1851), 142.

[19] Frank Soulé, John H. Gihon, and James Nisbet, *The Annals of San Francisco* (New York, 1855), 419–420.

stagnant pools, beset one at every stride ... eight people occupying what was only space for two."[20] In the early 'fifties, the city's water supply was the cause of frightening warnings. At first, the wells which were sunk in the area produced water so dirty that it was impossible for drinking. Before long, however, an adequate supply of pure water ended this danger.[21]

Probably the greatest threat came from rats. They were large and often ferocious. Ships had brought great numbers of them from five continents, and, once arrived, they thrived almost unmolested. Not until 1853 were enough cats and terriers imported to lower the rodent population to the average of other American towns of that period.[22] Filth meant fleas and lice. Numerous enough in San Francisco, these were found everywhere in the gold regions. Swarms of mosquitoes troubled Sacramento and its environs.

The element of change contributed to bad health. Many gold seekers had been accustomed to a sedentary life. Long, uncomfortable travel by land and sea, the change of food, climate, and water—all were less merciful than at present. Finally, the change from a less strenuous life to one of great exertion in the broiling sun, usually in impractical clothing which was often wet and infrequently changed, challenged many diseases.[23] At the time, the temptation to overwork was presented as a cause for sudden deaths. This exhaustion lowered a man's resistance to the ever-present threat of disease. Later, as gold seeking progressed to deep mining and burrowing, the beneficial effects of sun and fresh air were minimized.[24]

Not least was the simple factor of want. The dangerous implications of exhaustion might have been modified if food shortages had not existed. Also lacking were doctors, medicines, fuel, warm clothes, and proper housing. Until the late 'fifties, even San Francisco visitors complained of the crowded conditions in the small, drafty, and ramshackle hotels, which were, nevertheless, far the superiors of the miners' tents and bare cabins.

As bad as health conditions were, they could have been much worse. Indeed, it is a great wonder that they were not. In the early critical days California was spared a great smallpox plague which could have been

---

[20] Shaw, op. cit., 31, 176.

[21] William Redmond Ryan, Personal Adventures in Upper and Lower California in 1848–9 (2 vols., London, 1850), II, 246.

[22] J. D. Borthwick, Three Years in California (Edinburgh and London, 1857), 158–160.

[23] L. J. Hall, Around the Horn in '49 (Aboard the Henry Lee, 1849), 174.

[24] Franklin Tuthill, The History of California (San Francisco, 1866), 628.

catastrophic. The rat invasion brought no bubonic plague, and, apparently, the unchecked influx of Chinese, East Indians, and Hawaiians carried with it no serious consequences of Oriental illnesses. Leprosy was not a problem. Good climate could not have prevented such ills. California would have been almost helpless. That climate, however, did lighten the deadly harvests. In few other parts of the world could so improvident a gathering of humanity have survived so well as it did on the Pacific. In fact, nature seemed to counterbalance mankind's foolhardiness in favor of its welfare. As an observer noted,

Considering the very frequent use of pistols in San Francisco, it is a most providential circumstance that the climate is in a high degree favourable for the cure of gunshot wounds. These in general heal very rapidly, and many miraculous recoveries have taken place.[25]

In the interior, the dry air prevented the more rapid decay of costly foodstuffs, thereby saving much food from being wasted.

Numerous were the long-term results of the early illnesses. Physically, many victims were left weakened for life. Those who contracted dysentery were especially unfortunate, for injury to tissues of the colon was extensive and healing was almost always slow. Typhoid fever, too, often had serious aftereffects. Many invalids wandered from the diggings to San Francisco or Sacramento only to die on the streets or linger in some crowded, inadequate hospital. By disease, too, many gold hunters were dissuaded from continuing their precarious pursuit of "easy money." Samuel F. Wight summed up their attitude by turning to verse:

> The Chills and Fever, also, lent their aid,
> To shake my resolution, and persuade,
> A hesitating mind to delve no more,
> As Fortune had some better fate in store.[26]

Others, whose conclusions were less optimistic, returned to their old homes to give California the undeserved but shortlived reputation of a pesthole.

The most lasting result of the health tragedy was the commencement of organized efforts to make California what American visitors of the Mexican period had called it, a land of abundant health and strength. The story was a tedious one.

Even before the gold rush was fully under way, good health advice was given by honest observers. Unfortunately, it often went unheeded.

---

[25] Borthwick, *op. cit.*, 282–283.
[26] Samuel F. Wight, *Adventures in California and Nicaragua in Rhyme* (Boston, 1860), 38.

Authors of early tourist guides usually gave these warnings. Daniel B. Woods, solicitous for the welfare of western wanderers, had these words of his book put in bold-faced type: "BE CAREFUL OF YOUR HEALTH!" Woods was not so much concerned that the gold washer keep his feet dry while working as he was that the miner take care of himself in his leisure time, for he realized that to remain wet while not physically active was dangerous. He recommended, too, a midday rest, hoping thereby to save the miners from exhaustion. Common-sense personal care was his cardinal point. The incautious suffered, and Woods noticed that these were very often the most robust and vigorous who trusted their strength to prevent illness.[27]

The problem of proper clothing was elaborated upon by Frank Marryat, an English visitor of the time. He advised the men to wear flannel next to the skin. This, he admonished, should not be removed from the upper part of the body except for morning bathing. Such a precaution would lessen the threat of chest complaints. For those who worked in the rain, Marryat recommended the wearing of a blanket with a hole cut in its center for one's head, thus producing a poncho. He set himself strongly against the excessive use of medicines, a view which all advisers agreed upon. He told readers to throw away their medicine chests, which at best were "boxes of rubbish," always too dangerous for the novice. Having seen too many gold seekers dosing themselves with mercury at the first symptom of fever, he was disgusted with nostrums. To him, the only valuable medicines were quinine and castor oil. Correctly prescribing rest not only for disease prevention but as an aid in arresting fever, Marryat observed that this was often difficult for a proud person, for, he said, "the fear of the jeers of his healthier companions will often cause a man to continue work when prudence would dictate an opposite course."[28]

The diet problem concerned other self-appointed experts. These were no modern dieticians, but much of their advice was sound. Because of the likelihood of food poisoning, pork was advised against. Beef or fish should be substituted. Wheat meal, cheese, dried fruits, Indian corn meal, and rice could provide a fairly well-balanced diet, and, fortunately, one usually obtainable. Meat should be boiled rather than fried, one warned. Advisers generally agreed that alcohol, especially in warm weather, should be avoided. Theodore T. Johnson favored chocolate rather than the more common coffee and tea, probably for its soothing effect and

[27] Daniel B. Woods, *Sixteen Months at the Gold Diggings* (New York, 1851), 182–183.
[28] Frank Marryat, *Mountains and Molehills* (New York, 1855), 336–339.

nutritive value. He, too, was the enemy of strong medicine, believing in "the kindly efforts of Nature, assisted by proper regimen and diet."[29]

Carl Meyer, propagandist for a German emigration society, agreed with the rest that keeping warm would help ward off several diseases, but opposed the consumption of "too many juicy vegetables, such as melons, salads, radishes, etc," which, he believed, might cause dysentery. These vegetables, vital to scurvy victims, really needed thorough washing in pure water or proper cooking.[30]

Some of the gold seekers could profitably absorb vicarious knowledge. Most had to learn by experience. When illness struck, the California pioneer, at best, was cared for in a haphazard manner. The price of medicines matched those of most foodstuffs. Doctors' fees, too, were prohibitive. As a result, there was much self-doctoring. Dosing was resorted to, as has been mentioned, but usually the gold seeker worked until he could work no more. Then,

one morning . . . some one who has a "claim" near by has not appeared in the morning to dig as usual. Perhaps a miner, more benevolent than the rest, visits his tent and finds him seriously ill . . . a little attention is paid him, but the third morning he is found to be dead. No one knows him and he is hastily buried on the next hill.[31]

This was common if not typical. Nevertheless, some sick or disabled miners were saved through the generosity of their fellow gold seekers who paid their way home.[32]

Self-help and the kindly ministrations by mining-camp neighbors were poor substitutes for medical knowledge. Probably few real cures were achieved. Such crude care could have aroused little confidence, and unfortunately, that faith was misplaced. Americans of that time put much confidence in patent medicines and their prophets, the quacks. In California, where the sick were always desperate for any symbol of healing, many looked to these charlatans to make them whole. These men of single purpose came of varied background. Some had been barbers, lawyers, farmers, dishonored medical men, or general ne'er-do-wells.[33] A contemporary, William Kelly, describes the typical trappings of this pseudo-profession.

[29] Johnson, op. cit., 250.
[30] Carl Meyer, Prospectus to Form a Society for Emigration to California [1852], Ruth Frey Axe, trans. (Claremont, California, 1938), 11.
[31] Kip, op. cit., 87.
[32] Carr, op. cit., 112.
[33] Joseph W. Revere, Keel and Saddle (Boston, 1872), 169.

[They] roamed about, carrying a pair of saddle-bags, one side containing a select assortment of cutlery adapted either for trade or surgical uses, the other stored with a "beggarly array" of little boxes and flint vials . . . confined to calomel, castor-oil, and blue mass, which they administered in every ailment.[34]

Prescriptions varied, but fees seldom grew more reasonable. A German hairdresser championed bark tea as his panacea. Since he could peel his medicine from the near-by trees, the tea cost him nothing, but his patients paid five dollars![35] Even the most gullible do not have impregnable constitutions. Often the duped miners revolted against their tormentors. Some demanded to see the "doctor's" diploma. When this did not appear, the quack was given a warm exit.

In urban centers, the impostor adopted subtlety. Medicine being a mystery to even the best-informed layman, the idea of medical specialization usually drew the awe of the public. Therefore, quacks seldom deigned to style themselves general practitioners. Due to the local climate, catarrh and rheumatism were common; consequently, catarrh and rheumatic "specialists" thickly competed. More cautious than their brethren of the diggings, the San Francisco quacks sometimes provided themselves with genuine medical-school diplomas by offering to the widows of physicians and surgeons enough money to persuade some of the less scrupulous to sell their late husbands' diplomas![36] The next step was advertising. Some quacks composed their own propaganda, but others hired "broken down literary men . . . who will sell their talent for a glass of grog."[37] These ads filled the San Francisco papers throughout the period under discussion and for some time afterward. On the city's main street corners, boys passed out handbills, nailed placards on lampposts, threw others into carriages, and pushed their quack literature under front doors.

At first, capable doctors were scarce, but the middle 'fifties saw them come in greater numbers. In the gold fields, honorable medical men set up their tents, and, with the equipment available, did their best to relieve the sick. In the early part of this first decade, the doctors had organized medical fraternities, and soon had established medical journals. Often, these men·were fine products of the best colleges and universities of Europe and the eastern states. With this background, they were prepared to establish California's medical profession on an admirable foundation.[38]

[34] Kelly, op. cit., II, 151–152.

[35] Shaw, op. cit., 97.

[36] The Lancet, LVII (1849), 385.

[37] B. E. Lloyd, Lights and Shades in San Francisco (San Francisco, 1876), 445–446.

[38] Probably the best work on California's medical profession is Henry Harris, California's Medical Story (San Francisco, 1932).

In these early days, doctors were both difficult and expensive to summon. The sick needed emergency care. It had to be treatment *en masse,* thus hospitals were indispensable. The federal government led by founding in 1852 the best hospital San Francisco was to have in the 'fifties. This was the United States Marine Hospital, so much admired that it became an attraction for early travelers. Even those most critical of other hospitals vouched for its cleanliness and adequate facilities. The death rate there, even for the perilous year 1853, was surprisingly low and decreased rapidly thereafter.[39]

The state provided a less successful institution, the State Marine Hospital. In 1855, an investigating committee, visiting its premises in San Francisco, found that the state was paying $1,470 monthly for the same building which earlier had been offered to other parties for $400 a month. The institution was almost immediately abolished, and the counties were encouraged to support their own sick by a poll tax or personal tax.[40]

In San Francisco, municipal attempts to provide hospitals were no less a fiasco. Indeed, the notoriety of the City Hospital was perpetuated by several writers. In 1849, the city made contracts with private groups who were to care for the indigent sick. Of the five dollars provided for the care of each destitute sick person, much was pocketed by the early administrators. The wards were crowded and the nurses rough and vulgar. Coffins seem to have been the only plentiful item, and they were filled at the rate of three a day.[41] Sacramento, Stockton, and Sonora had their early hospitals, but only that of Sacramento was nearly adequate.

Ministers, through their good works, had more success. They brought to the public's attention the conditions of the hospitals and the activities of quacks. In San Francisco, many Methodists and Baptists were spared the need of resorting to public hospitals; their brethren cared for them, sometimes in their own homes. Congregations raised large sums to pay the homeward passage of their sick co-religionists. Not only did money flow freely in the churches where ministers made frequent pleas, but even camp meetings held in the Plaza collected substantial funds for the fares of destitute invalids.[42]

The Roman Catholics had their own hospital, conducted by the Sisters of Mercy. Twenty nuns cared for an average of twenty patients a month.

[39] Henry G. Langley and Samuel A. Mathews, compilers, *The State Register, and Year Book of Facts for the Year 1857* (San Francisco, 1857), 49, 150.
[40] Theodore H. Hittell, *History of California* (4 vols., San Francisco, 1898), IV, 163.
[41] Taylor, *op. cit.,* 220.
[42] *Ibid.,* 228.

By 1861, the order had moved into a new and larger building which could accommodate 108 patients.[43]

Religious groups were rivaled in philanthropy by fraternal organizations. The Masons established a San Francisco lodge in October, 1849, and in less than a decade could boast the expenditure of several hundred thousand dollars for the relief of the sick and destitute. In Sacramento, the Masons and Odd Fellows were active. Cholera having broken out in 1850, fraternity members joined in caring for the sick and burying the dead.[44]

Ties of blood and homeland early united California's foreign immigrants in benevolent societies organized primarily for a form of health insurance. Regular dues were paid and medical care was provided. The French, Germans, Italians, Swiss, Jews, Scandinavians, and Chinese had their own mutual benefit societies.

By the 1860's, California health had seen a transformation. With the establishment of a more sedentary life and the growth of agriculture and the appearance of more material conveniences, health statistics showed the fast decline of the terrible epidemics of the 'fifties.[45] Heart disease now became the important malady which puzzled doctors as well as the general public. Perhaps this illness symbolized the times, for heart disease is usually prominent in settled societies. Indeed, the prevailing illnesses had changed. California had changed from a mining frontier to a more agricultural state. Sanitation replaced filth. Transportation succeeded difficult communication and accelerated the development of good medical facilities. In a decade, everything had changed but the climate. That climate was to be paramount in a new westward movement. California was on the threshold of a "health rush," a longer, slower, yet greater immigration seeking a mightier lure than gold, that of life itself.

---

[43] Henry G. Langley, compiler, *The San Francisco Directory* (San Francisco, 1858), 389.

[44] H. S. Crocker, compiler, *The Sacramento Directory, 1871* (Sacramento, 1871), 78.

[45] Joseph Weed, *A View of California as It Is* (San Francisco, 1874), 126.

Mining Methods in Catgut Cañon

EDWIN H. CARPENTER, JR.

ALTHOUGH it was the Washoe silver rush rather than the California gold rush in which Mark Twain personally took part, his broad interests and his visits to the Sierra foothills in 1865–1866, when there were still plenty of old-timers living in the shrunken mining camps, created in him a sympathy for the men and the *mores* of '49. Since he had some direct experience with mineral extraction, the announcement in 1880 of a novel method of procuring gold evoked the following satiric squib about the techniques he had known in his California days.

As a research assistant to Dr. Dixon Wecter, editor of the Mark Twain Papers, the undersigned found this item in the files belonging to the Samuel L. Clemens Estate, with whose consent it is here reprinted. The closing remark is a reference to the fact that Winfield Scott Hancock, the Democratic presidential nominee in 1880, had been a Union general, in large degree responsible for the northern victory at Gettysburg.

❖ ❖ ❖

GOLD IN SOLUTION

Alleged Remarkable Yield of the Metal

San Francisco, September 11.—A despatch from Calistoga, Napa county, says: Excitement has existed in this neighborhood for the last fortnight over a report that the Hot Springs in this place carry large quantities of gold in solution. A. C. Tichenor, who recently bought the Hot Springs Hotel property, has been at work for the last two weeks extracting gold from the water by a process known only to himself. The clear up yesterday afternoon showed that he has succeeded in extracting $1,060 from ten barrels of water. The gold is of the utmost fineness, and as the springs in the locality are many in number, the volume of water is exceedingly large. It would be useless to attempt to estimate their value, if they continue to yield as rich a return as the experiments thus far have proved.

—New York *Evening Post*, September 14, 1880

"MILLIONS IN IT"

Mark Twain on the Gold-Bearing Water—How
he Worked the Calistoga Springs and What he
Knows About a Wonderful Gold-Bearing Wind

To the Editors of the Evening Post:

I have just seen your despatch from San Francisco, in Saturday's EVE-NING POST, about "Gold in Solution" in the Calistoga Springs, and about the proprietor's having "extracted $1,060 in gold of the utmost fineness from ten barrels of water" during the past fortnight, by a process known only to himself. This will surprise many of your readers, but it does not surprise me, for I once owned those springs myself. What does surprise me, however, is the falling off in the richness of the water. In my time the yield was a dollar a dipperful. I am not saying this to injure the property, in case a sale is contemplated. I am only saying it in the interest of history. It may be that this hotel proprietor's process is an inferior one—yes, that may be the fault. Mine was to take my uncle—I had an extra uncle at that time, on account of his parents dying and leaving him on my hands—and fill him up, and let him stand fifteen minutes to give the water a chance to settle well, then insert him in an exhausted receiver, which had the effect of sucking the gold out through his pores. I have taken more than eleven thousand dollars out of that old man in a day and a half. I should have held on to those springs but for the badness of the roads and the difficulty of getting the gold to market.

I consider that gold-yielding water in many respects remarkable; and yet not more remarkable than the gold bearing air of Catgut Canon, up there toward the head of the auriferous range. This air—or this wind—for it is a kind of a trade wind which blows steadily down through six hundred miles of rich quartz croppings during an hour and a quarter every day except Sundays, is heavily charged with exquisitely fine and impalpable gold. Nothing precipitates and solidifies this gold so readily as contact with human flesh heated by passion. The time that William Abrahams was disappointed in love, he used to step out doors when that wind was blowing, and come in again and begin to sigh, and his brother Andover J. would extract over a dollar and a half out of every sigh he sighed, right along. And the time that John Harbison and Aleck Norton quarrelled about Harbison's dog, they stood there swearing at each other all they knew how—and what they didn't know about swearing they couldn't learn from you and me, not by a good deal—and at the end of every three or four minutes they had to stop and make a dividend—if they didn't their jaws would clog up so that they couldn't get the big nine syllabled ones out at all—and when the wind was done blowing they cleaned up just a little over sixteen hundred dollars apiece. I know these facts to be absolutely true, because I got them from a man whose mother I knew personally. I do not suppose a person could buy a water privilege at Calistoga now at any price; but several good locations along the course of the Catgut Canon Gold-Bearing Trade-Wind are for sale. They are going to be stocked for the New York market. They will sell, too; the people will swarm for them as thick as Hancock veterans—in the South.

MARK TWAIN

Hartford, Conn., September 14, 1880.

—New York *Evening Post,* September 17, 1880